HEARTS

HEARTS

THE GOLDEN YEARS

TOM PURDIE

AMBERLEY

First published 2012

Amberley Publishing
The Hill, Stroud
Gloucestershire, GL5 4EP

www.amberley-books.com

British Library Cataloguing in Publication Data.
A catalogue record for this book is available from the British Library.

ISBN 978 1 4456 1078 8

Typeset in 10pt on 13pt Sabon.
Typesetting and Origination by Amberley Publishing.
Printed in the UK.

CONTENTS

ACKNOWLEDGEMENTS

I would like to express my thanks to the following for their assistance in the making of this book: *Edinburgh Evening News*, Campbell McCutcheon and Louis Archard of Amberley Publishing, Gary Kirk, Bob Laird, Eric McCowat, Alan Dick, David Macmillan, and Tom Wright, Hibs historian and curator of Hibernian Historical Trust. Special thanks to Andrew Hoggan and Heart of Midlothian's historian David Speed for their expertise and giving up valuable time to deal with my endless queries. Special thanks also to Hearts legends Jimmy Murray and Freddie Glidden for providing me with an insight into this era from a player's perspective.

Thanks are also due to my good friend and former Hearts player and manager, John Robertson, for writing such an excellent foreword.

FOREWORD

The very mention of the name Heart of Midlothian Football Club is one that immediately makes me smile and my heart swell with pride to know that I have been part of its proud history and traditions since they were founded in 1874.

Early success was forthcoming and League titles and Scottish Cups soon bore the famous maroon-and-white colours. The club was one of the leading lights as Scottish Football started to develop and no one will ever forget the ultimate sacrifice made by the Hearts team that joined McCrae's Battalion in the First World War while leading the Scottish First Division.

Many great players both past and present have played their part in representing this famous club and all deserve their place in the history and fabric of Heart of Midlothian FC.

The 1950s to 1960s period that this book covers and takes for its title, 'The Golden Years', was exactly that, for this was the period and these were the players that became the standard bearers for all future Hearts players to strive to reach; a team that swept all before them, winning League titles and Scottish and League cups with a style and panache that would see them herald the most celebrated and successful time in the club's history.

Led by manager Tommy Walker, the names still roll off the tongue: Dave Mackay, Alec Young, Freddie Glidden, John Cumming, Alfie Conn, Jimmy Wardhaugh, Willie Bauld and so many more gave Hearts eight years of memories, trophies and feats that will not be repeated any time soon, if ever. League titles in 1958 and 1960, the 1956 Scottish Cup, Scottish League Cups in 1954, 1958, 1959 and 1962... Who at that time would think it would be thirty-six years before silverware was once more seen in Gorgie Road?

The League title of 1958 was incredible, with a sensational sixty-two points and 132 goals scored, with only one defeat as the all-conquering team swept through to the title.

This was the team that set the bar, set the standard and gave all Hearts fans the reason to believe in the club, the reason to believe that once more we could and would compete at the top level. It was this era that defined the football club and established Hearts as the biggest club in Scotland outwith the Old Firm.

For those fortunate enough to see this era it was the pinnacle of the club's history to date, an era filled with great football and goals galore and men who are real

Tom Purdie and John Robertson.

'Legends', a term bestowed far too easily these days on players who simply could not lace the boots of the players from this time.

When I joined the club in 1981 it was this team I wanted to emulate, their success I wanted to achieve as I believed if we could win it then, we could win it now. I wanted to try and reach the standards of my late father's heroes, the men he spoke fondly of and the stories he told of their great games and skills. It was a dream not quite fulfilled but the challenge was there and it is a challenge that all current and future Hearts teams and players should strive to equal.

I know the pride and honour that Tom Purdie has in putting this book together and it is exactly what it says in the title – 'The Golden Years', a time when Hearts' history and records were rewritten and its place in Scottish Football cemented forever.

John Robertson
(Former Hearts player and manager, and Scotland international)

INTRODUCTION

Some years ago I had a book published named *Scottish Football – The Golden Years* which reflected on football in Scotland during the 1950s and 60s. During that period the game experienced huge attendances and fans enjoyed watching teams in which skill abounded. Teams outwith Rangers and Celtic such as Dundee, Clyde, Motherwell, Partick Thistle, Kilmarnock, Hearts and Hibernian were packed with talent, even the now departed but fondly remembered Third Lanark, to name but a few. Clyde had Archie Robertson, Tommy Ring and George Herd; Motherwell produced the 'Ancell Babes' of Reid, Quinn, St John, Hunter and Weir; Dundee, the quite brilliant strike force of the two Alans, Cousin and Gilzean. Hearts of course had 'the Terrible Trio' of Conn, Bauld and Wardhaugh, who made goalscoring seem easy; meanwhile their city rivals, Hibernian, had the 'Famous Five' of Smith, Johnstone, Reilly, Turnbull and Ormond. Who can forget the wing wizardry of Jimmy Johnstone and Willie Henderson or the magnificent Jim Baxter, one of the finest players I have ever seen grace a football field – how well we remember Jim's virtuoso performances at Wembley in 1963 and 1967 against the 'Auld Enemy' – Aberdeen's Graham Leggat, Celtic's Willie Fernie, Kilmarnock's Brian McIlroy, Third Lanark's Dave Hilley, Gerry Baker and Tommy Bryceland of St Mirren, Jimmy McEwan, Raith Rovers... The list is endless. Each of these players along with many others were household names in Scotland.

In that time it wasn't just Rangers and Celtic who won all the honours as Aberdeen, Clyde, Dunfermline, Hearts, Falkirk, Dundee, East Fife, Motherwell and St Mirren were successful in either the Scottish Cup, the League Cup or in some cases both. The League Championship was won by Aberdeen, Hibernian, Hearts, Dundee and Kilmarnock. As a boy I grew up with these teams and their players and never ceased to be amazed by some of the talent in the game back then. To be honest, myself and others began to take for granted the footballing skills on display and it is only in later years when you reflect that you realise what a privilege it was to have been there to see those players in action. Yes, there were poor games at times and yes Baxter and co. were more than capable of having their off days as well as anybody else, but by and large it was a great time to watch football.

As a kid, any game you had been to see was always re-enacted in the days following the match. This would inevitably take place on a piece of waste ground with jackets or coats acting as makeshift goalposts as, along with your pals, you tried to emulate your footballing heroes. There was no offside in these encounters, which could often result in a 16-16 draw or a 19-18 victory, and games usually lasted until the sun went down. We refereed the games ourselves and applied the rules of the game quite loosely, the final decisions always being made by someone whose name was prefixed by 'Big'. So it was always 'Big Wull', 'Big John' or 'Big Geordie' who said 'Naw, it wiz by the post' or 'Penalty' and the most important one, 'Aye that's a goal'. Never was it 'Wee Shug', 'Wee Eck' or 'Wee Airchie' who got to make these vital decisions.

But it was also a great era to grow up in and life seemed so simple and uncomplicated back then when playing, watching and reading about football took up a large part of our lives. Every Christmas you hoped that one of your presents would be *The Scottish Football Book*, which was written by Hugh Taylor and cost 10s 6d. It was first published in 1955 before being discontinued in 1980. It was a treasure trove of information and photographs about the Scottish game and was read cover to cover over and over again. Another 'must' was the *Wee Red Book* football handbook, which was published by the *Glasgow Evening Times* newspaper. The first publication was in the early 1930s and initially it was given free with the newspaper. It cost 3d when it came back into circulation after the Second World War but by 1957 it had increased in price to 6d. It came out just before the start of the football season and established an informative directory of all the senior clubs in Scotland. Packed with information regarding players, individual club records, league tables and various trophy winners etc., along with all the forthcoming fixtures, it was well worth the money. It is still in circulation but now costs substantially more.

Very few people had cars and nearly everyone travelled by bus or train, which always seemed to arrive on time. Milk and newspapers were delivered to your home on a daily basis, the Royal Mail made a morning and afternoon visit every day except Sundays, 'Elf 'n' Safety' wasn't applied so rigorously as it is today and 'Yuman Rites' and 'Political Correctness' hadn't been heard of. The streets were friendly with that 'go next door and borrow some milk' neighbourliness; people cared for each other, well, apart from the occasional Saturday night when the pubs came out. There were butchers, bakers, grocers and newsagent shops and you were spoiled for choice when it came to fish and chip shops. Saturdays couldn't come quick enough and you practically wished your life away when you uttered the words 'I wish it was Saturday'. We grew up without iPads, Blackberrys, iPhones etc., but we had PlayStations; we called them football fields.

Some people may argue that the Baxters, the Bakers, Hendersons and Johnstones wouldn't survive in today's game. Oh yeah? In the playing days of the aforementioned, the ball was heavy and that was on dry days. On wet days it weighed the equivalent of a ton while the playing surfaces were on occasions compatible with paddy fields and were a long way short of the playing areas which the players of today enjoy. Today's modern game is now almost a non-contact sport, with nearly every tackle being penalised. In those guys' playing days some of the tackles were akin to assault, so you can imagine how good they would be now, given the amount of protection players are afforded in the modern game.

The Scottish international side also carried an array of talent such as Denis Law, Bobby Collins, Jackie Mudie, John White and Bobby Evans. TV coverage of football was still in its infancy but when it eventually came into our living rooms on a regular basis on a Saturday night, you wouldn't have missed it for the world. There was nothing better in the long winter evenings than to sit by the fireside with its blazing coal fire and the living room curtains drawn waiting for the BBC's *Sportsreel* or STV's *Scotsport* to appear on your parents' black-and white-television set. It was something else to listen to Arthur Montford's commentaries on Scotsport. Arthur had the ability to make even the most turgid of games sound exciting as he exclaimed, 'UP GO THE HEADS' or 'CHANCE OF A LIFETIME' followed by 'WHAT A STRAMASH'. But the one most remembered was the inevitable 'DISASTER FOR SCOTLAND' as the national side once again managed to snatch a defeat from the jaws of victory.

As a youngster my friends and I would select what we thought was the best game to watch that particular Saturday afternoon and once the selection was made, after some quite lengthy debate, we would set off by public transport to the agreed venue, where on arrival a match programme just had to be purchased. Some of the grounds were very Spartan, almost 'Dickensian', with little or no cover from the elements apart from in the main stands, which were cost-prohibitive to my friends and myself. Then it was time to go through the turnstiles. We always went through the 'boys' gate' as this mode of entry was considerably cheaper. If my memory serves me correctly, I'm sure that one had to be under sixteen years of age to gain entry at the reduced price. The turnstile attendants always looked identical, irrespective of which ground you were at. They all wore the same look on their faces – authoritative, surly and suspicious – and inevitably had the same attire, a bulky overcoat and a flat cap. This seemed to be the accepted uniform of turnstile operators throughout the land. The attendants scrutinised your face in a manner that would normally only be reserved for some fugitive on the wanted list of the FBI before grumpily asking the question 'Whit age 'ur you son?' Naturally an age was provided that would go some way in satisfying his curiosity. A further in-depth look at your features would take place before he would click the turnstile to allow entry. Honestly, some of those guys could have performed duties admirably alongside the East German guards who manned the Berlin Wall at that time. There were usually six or seven of us in the group, which included fans of Rangers, Celtic, Hearts and Hibs so you can well imagine the arguments which ensued between us, as the game chosen had to involve one of the teams we followed. Each of us had a favourite ground on our travels and my particular one was Broomfield, the home of Airdrieonians. Not because of the atmosphere in the ground or the pies on sale there or anything else pertaining to football. No, it was much simpler than that. My uncle Harry was a policeman in Airdrie Burgh Police, as it was known then, and often performed match-day duties at Broomfield. If the occasion arose that Airdrie was the selected venue, uncle Harry saw to it that me and my pals were allowed through a 'special' gate free of charge which made us feel important, similar to VIPs. Every time this happened my 'street cred' jumped another few notches in the eyes of my friends. It was a sad day for me when uncle Harry transferred to the CID and no longer patrolled Broomfield.

The memorial to the Hearts of Midlothian players and members who fell in the Great War was unveiled at the Haymarket on 9 April 1922 by Secretary of State for Scotland Robert Munro KC MP. The crowd, thought to be about 35,000, heard him say, 'Hearts had shown on the battlefield that courage, resource, skill, endurance, dash and daring that made them famous on the football field. Thank God for men like the Hearts players who fell in the morning of their days and saved the British people from destruction'.

One day a new lad and his family, who were from Fife, moved into our housing scheme, nowadays called estates. He was found to be 'OK' and asked if he could become part of our 'team'. We were all set to take him on board when we discovered to our horror that the football side he followed was Cowdenbeath. We felt that it was taking things to the extreme, the possibility of us having to watch Cowdenbeath, and his request for enrolment was denied. Even the fact that he had an older sister who was absolutely gorgeous and that his father owned a car could not make us overturn the decision.

I watched Hearts playing on numerous times in those days and marvelled at the tenacity of a Dave Mackay tackle, the graceful skills of Alex Young, the heading ability of Willie Bauld and I still look back on those days with fond affection. As a

This photograph of the memorial was taken on Remembrance Sunday 1948.

result I decided to compile this book using programmes and photographs to look back on what I consider to be the 'Golden Years' of this famous side and to highlight various games of importance during that era. I have also referred to newspaper reports of some games to remind the older fans how football journalism has changed and to also give them an opportunity to reflect on the game's past while providing younger fans with an opportunity to read about footballers from a bygone era.

I've had the pleasure of meeting and enjoying the company of some of the legends who played back then – Gordon Marshall, Willie Duff, Bobby Kirk, Andy Bowman, Bobby Parker, Freddie Glidden, Dave Mackay, John Cumming, Johnny Hamilton, Jimmy Murray, Danny Paton and Alex Young – so it gives me a great deal of satisfaction to write about their deeds in the hope that it keeps the memory of their achievements alive.

Over the years nearly everyone had a 'soft spot' for Heart of Midlothian for a variety of reasons. In the years between the First World War and Second World War, Hearts had endeavoured to play good football and although they had not won the trophies their style of play deserved, they continued to play with spirit and in a sporting manner which caught the public's eye. The sporting press from those days always highlighted this when referring to Hearts as they had always been associated with all that was best in football entertainment. Their popularity also evolved round the First World War. Heart of Midlothian were admired by the nation when, just after the outbreak of the Great War in 1914, the majority of the team volunteered to serve their country, going from the playing fields of Scotland to the killing fields of France, where the side was decimated. When the guns fell silent in 1918, some returned to Gorgie to once again pull on the famous maroon jersey and run onto the field to the roar of the crowd. Others returned but because of their wounds, injuries and mental scars were unable to play again; some didn't return at all.

When Hearts began to win the prizes their play so richly deserved, very few people begrudged them the success. This is their story.

HEARTS – THE GOLDEN YEARS

Saturday 23 October 1954 was a dank and dreary wet afternoon in the city of Glasgow. Dismal it may have been, but not for the thousands of Hearts fans standing on the vast slopes of Hampden Park who had just witnessed their team defeat Motherwell 4-2 in the final of the Scottish League Cup, the first major trophy the club had won since defeating Third Lanark 1-0 in the 1905/06 Scottish Cup final. As captain Bobby Parker held the trophy aloft to the resounding cheers of the Hearts support within Hampden, little did the fans back then know that this was to be the beginning of the most successful period in the club's history, 1954 till 1962, in which Hearts would go on to win the League Championship twice, 1957/58 and 1959/60, the League Cup on three more occasions, 1958/59, 1959/60, 1962/63, and the Scottish Cup in 1955/56. They would also be runners-up in the League twice, 1956/57 and 1958/59, and finalists in the 1961/62 League Cup. European football would also come to Tynecastle in seasons 1958/59, 1960/61 and 1961/62.

For many years Hearts had become the 'nearly team', never really fulfilling expectations, and as a result became the butt of music hall jokes up and down the country. A comedian had only to say, 'Is this going to be Hearts' year at last?' and the audience would fall about helpless with laughter. What was the problem with Hearts? Bad luck? Lack of the 'killer instinct'? Whatever it was, some people had a quiet laugh at Hearts' misfortunes, though they had a measure of sympathy for the famous old club. But all that was about to change as manager Tommy Walker formed a formidable side that was to become feared throughout Scottish football, drawing massive attendances as thousands flocked to see them at home and away. He began to build a team combining artistry and determination, resulting in attacking football and resolute defending. Walker had returned to Hearts after an eighteen-month spell with Chelsea, and after the untimely death of manager David McLean on 14 February 1951 he took over the mantle of manager. The 1954 League Cup triumph was the catalyst for a period in the history of the Heart of Midlothian which is unlikely to be repeated.

Season 1951/52 was Walker's first full term in charge at Tynecastle but Hearts failed to qualify for the final stages of the League Cup and finished in fourth place in the League Championship. To add insult to injury their great rivals from across the city, Hibernian, had finished as Champions, ten points ahead of them. They did however reach the semi-finals of the Scottish Cup, but lost 3-1 to Motherwell after

The programme for the opening League Cup game against Rangers on 9 August 1952. Goals by Conn (2), Wardhaugh (2) and Bauld got Hearts off to the perfect start before 41,000 spectators. This was the first issue of a new-style programme introduced by the club and was one of the best in circulation among Scottish clubs at that time. Among the contents were messages of good wishes from manager Tommy Walker to John Harvey, who had stepped up as chief trainer, and his assistant Donald McLeod. The programme carried various adverts, one of which was for the Tynecastle Arms public house, which encouraged one to partake of 'a glass of ale midst fellow supporters before and after the match' and another for Tommy's Cafe at 4 Orwell Place, where lunch was being served between 12 and 2.30 p.m.

two 1-1 draws. It is interesting to note that these three games attracted 238,044 spectators through the Hampden turnstiles, with the gate receipts amounting to £16,560. It was little or no consolation to Hearts that Motherwell went on to defeat Dundee 4-0 in the final.

Would the following season of 1952/53 change all that and bring good fortune to the long-suffering fans? It certainly seemed that way as Hearts got off to a blistering start by beating Rangers 5-0 in the opening League Cup sectional tie at Tynecastle. This was followed by another impressive display at Pittodrie in mid-week, as Walker's men ran out 4-2 winners against Aberdeen. Hearts were four goals up at the interval through Bauld (2), Parker (pen.) and Rutherford before Ewen and Yorston for the 'Dons' made the scoreline more respectable. However, the other team in the section, Motherwell, brought Hearts back to earth by beating them 1-0 in Gorgie the following Saturday. A week later Rangers exacted revenge by winning 2-0 at Ibrox in front of over 70,000. The League Cup dream was effectively over and again they failed to qualify for the final stages of the competition, finishing in second place in their section.

The League campaign began with a victory over Third Lanark at Cathkin Park but erratic form throughout the remainder of the season saw Hearts finish once again in fourth place, with thirty points.

The Scottish Cup brought fresh hope and after defeating Raith Rovers, Montrose and Queen of the South, they faced Rangers in the semi-final at Hampden. Would the Edinburgh men succeed this time?

In front of a crowd of 116,262, they got off a great start to the game when Wardhaugh scored after eleven minutes. For long periods of the game Hearts dominated and they seemed destined to reach their first Scottish Cup final in forty-six years. Was 'Lady Luck' shining on them at long last, their fans asked? The answer to that question arrived eight minutes from the break when Rangers' Grierson took advantage of a defensive error by the Hearts rearguard and equalised. But at the start of the second half Hearts remained optimistic and continued to play well. Maybe 'Lady Luck' was still there? With twenty-five minutes remaining and the

Right: Programme for the 1953 Scottish Cup semi-final against Rangers.

Below: Scottish Cup semi-final, 4 April 1953. Eleven minutes gone and Jimmy Wardhaugh puts Hearts into the lead.

Above: Lucky Rangers as this shot from Jimmy Wardhaugh strikes the post with Rangers' George Niven helpless in the 1952/53 Scottish Cup semi-final.

Left: Programme for Hearts *v.* Rangers League Cup game, 26 August 1953. It was a game Hearts needed to win to stay in contention for the final stages of the competition. After leading for much of the game by virtue of a Willie Bauld goal, Derek Grierson equalised for Rangers with twelve minutes to go. The front cover of the programme had now changed from the previous season and featured an action-shot photograph from previous games. It cost 3*d* and was excellent value for the twelve-page publication. Among the adverts inside was one from British Railways giving times for their Football Specials for the Raith Rovers *v.* Hearts game on 29 August. Leaving from Piershill at 11.40 a.m., the train would call at Abbeyhill, Waverley and Haymarket, arriving in Kirkcaldy at 1.10 p.m., and the fare was 2*s* 9*d* return.

game balanced at 1-1, she decided to move on. John Cumming went down injured and for the remainder of the match became a virtual passenger. But could Hearts still hold on and force a replay? You could almost hear the 'Lady' whispering, 'Aye right'. The Glasgow side took full advantage of Cumming's injury and with fifteen minutes to go scored what can only be described as a fortuitous goal, when a shot from Prentice of Rangers took a deflection off Hearts defender John Adie and ended up in the net. 'Lady Luck' had well and truly 'left the building'. So once again the support made the long way back along the main Glasgow to Edinburgh A8 road with heavy hearts and once more it was of no consolation that Rangers would win the trophy by overcoming Aberdeen in the final. Despite their brand of attacking play, Hearts still collapsed at the vital games. But Walker and his back-room side were not despondent, as they knew that one day good football would triumph.

When the 1953/54 season got underway Hearts were grouped in their League Cup section with Hamilton Academical, Raith Rovers and Rangers. It was obvious that to qualify they had to overcome the Glasgow giants. In front of 27,064 fans they put Hamilton Accies to the sword in a 5-0 demolition, the 'Terrible Trio' of Conn, Bauld and Wardhaugh sharing the goals. The next fixture saw them face Rangers at Ibrox and after only ten minutes of play they found themselves two goals down. Bauld scored just before the break but another two goals by Rangers in the final six minutes put paid to any hope of victory. Hearts failed to qualify for the quarter-final stages of the tournament, finishing in second place behind Rangers. Their early League form was disappointing but they began putting some fine performances together, including victories over the 'Old Firm' and Hibs both home and away. Very soon Hearts were mounting a serious challenge to become League champions. However, injuries to key players began to take their toll and a string of poor results coming towards the end of the season saw them finish in second place behind Champions Celtic.

In between, a trip to Fraserburgh in the Scottish Cup saw Hearts progress to the next round with a 3-0 win. The contest was played in gale force winds and driving rain but it wasn't without humour. After coming off the field, blue with the cold, the players were given brochures exhorting them to 'come to Fraserburgh for your holidays'. The squad stayed overnight in Aberdeen and that evening took a trip to the cinema to watch Kenneth More, Kay Kendall, John Gregson and Dinah Sheridan starring in *Genevieve*. Queen of the South were disposed of 2-1 at Palmerston in the following round but a 3-0 defeat at the hands of Aberdeen in the quarter-finals finished the dream of Cup glory.

But the 'Gorgie Faithful' had a right to feel a bit more satisfied with their team's overall performance, as this had been Hearts' highest placing in the League since 1937/38, when they had finished in second place to Celtic by three points. So what would 1954/55 bring? It would bring glory back to Tynecastle and see Hearts embark on a period in their history which was most certainly the 'Golden Years'. It would bring unbridled joy to the long-suffering support as thousands flocked to the famous old ground to see their heroes in maroon as the team imposed themselves emphatically on Scottish football, no more to be described as one of the most mercurial sides in Scotland.

SEASON 1954/55

THE LEAGUE CUP

During the close season Hearts had travelled to South Africa, having been invited to take part in a tour involving ten games. They returned to Edinburgh at the end of June having lost only one game, a 2-1 reversal by South Africa in Durban. The month-long trip seemed to have paid dividends as they defeated Dundee 3-1 in the opening League Cup sectional tie. Also in the section were Celtic and Falkirk. Out of the six games played they lost only one and qualified for the quarter-final stages, where they were drawn against Second Division St Johnstone. The Perth men were swept aside in the two-legged encounter, 5-0 and 2-0. The semi-final draw saw Hearts travel the short distance across the capital to Easter Road to face Airdrieonians. Despite conceding a goal early in the game Hearts ran out 4-1 winners and proceeded to the final, where they would meet Motherwell at Hampden Park on 23 October. Manager Tommy Walker realised the Motherwell side would be difficult opponents, having disposed of the much-fancied Rangers in the quarter-finals and beating the previous year's winners, East Fife, in the other semi-final, and so would field his strongest side.

THE LEAGUE CUP FINAL 1954/55

The 'Maroon Faithful' made their way to Glasgow in great numbers and despite the poor weather a crowd of over 55,000 turned out to watch the game. The team line-ups were:

Hearts: Duff, Parker, Mackenzie, Mackay, Glidden, Cumming, Souness, Conn, Bauld, Wardhaugh, Urquhart.

Motherwell: Weir, Kilmarnock, McSeveney, Cox, Paton, Redpath, Hunter, Aitken, Bain, Humphries, Williams.

Saturday night's *Edinburgh Evening Dispatch* carried the following report of the game:

> Every Heart was a hero at Hampden today and Willie Bauld was magnificent. He scored three of the Maroons' four goals. Wardhaugh headed home the other. The Tynecastle crowd raised a cheer when Tom Mackenzie, pronounced fit, took the field

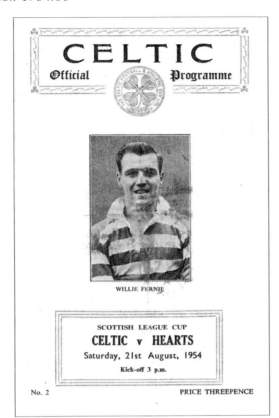

WILLIE FERNIE

SCOTTISH LEAGUE CUP

CELTIC v HEARTS

Saturday, 21st August, 1954

Kick-off 3 p.m.

No. 2   PRICE THREEPENCE

Right: The programme for the 2-1 victory over Celtic at Celtic Park on 21 August 1954, featuring Willie Fernie of Celtic on the front cover.

Below, left and right: The programmes for Hearts' 6-2 win at Brockville on 18 August and the 4-1 defeat by Dundee at Dens Park on 28 August 1954. The programmes cost threepence and are now very rare, as are the majority of match-day publications from that era.

AITKEN'S BEER

JUST WHAT I WANT!

FALKIRK F.C. LIMITED

SCOTTISH LEAGUE CUP — DIVISION A

Season 1954-55   No. 1

FALKIRK v HEARTS

WEDNESDAY, 18th, AUGUST 1954   KICK-OFF 7.15 p.m.

OFFICIAL PROGRAMME - - - THREEPENCE

THIS MAY BE **YOUR** LUCKY NUMBER AND MAY WIN YOU A PRIZE AT HALF-TIME   809

Telephone — Falkirk 1652
CARTNER & SANTI
JOINERS AND WOODWORKERS
HOWGATE :: FALKIRK
All classes of work executed. Estimates given free.

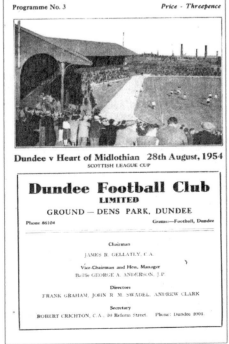

Programme No. 3   *Price - Threepence*

Dundee v Heart of Midlothian   28th August, 1954
SCOTTISH LEAGUE CUP

Dundee Football Club
LIMITED
GROUND — DENS PARK, DUNDEE

Phone 86104   Grams:—Football, Dundee

Chairman
JAMES R. GELLATLY, C.A.

Vice-Chairman and Hon. Manager
Bailie GEORGE A. ANDERSON, J.P.

Directors
FRANK GRAHAM, JOHN R. M. SWADEL, ANDREW CLARK

Secretary
ROBERT CRICHTON, C.A., 29 Reform Street.   Phone: Dundee 2001.

Marathon champion Joe McGhee being introduced to Willie Duff by Bobby Parker at Brockville before the League Cup game on 18 August 1954. Willie Duff had made his competitive debut for Hearts four days previously against Dundee at Tynecastle in the opening game of the tournament. Willie joined Hearts in August 1952 from junior side Easthouses Lily and was virtually a constant in the team, making thirty-nine appearances in 1954/55, and in the 1955/56 season he played forty-two competitive games. Due to him being called up for National Service, joining the Royal Horse Artillery, his appearances for Hearts in 1956/57 were restricted to four. His last competitive game was on 13 October 1956 at Tynecastle in a 5-2 defeat by East Fife. During his spell in the army Willie played for Charlton Athletic and consequently signed for the London club in January 1958. Duff joined Peterborough in 1963 and after four years there he returned north of the border in 1967 when George Farm, the Dunfermline manager, brought him to East End Park. On 27 April 1968 the Fifers met Hearts in the final of the Scottish Cup but Willie picked up an injury before the game and missed out on a winners' medal as Dunfermline beat his old side 3-1. What a fairy-tale ending that would have been for the 'keeper, who was nearing the end of his career. Willie and his family emigrated to the USA but after some years there he returned to his native Scotland. Sadly, Willie passed away on 30 August 2004.

Opposite above: Celtic's Charlie Tully watches the ball go over the bar. The Hearts players are Freddie Glidden, Willie Duff and John Adie, with Willie Fernie of Celtic.

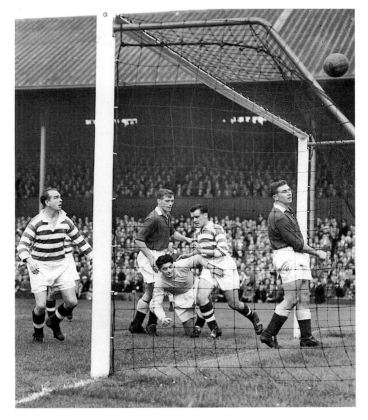

Below, left and right: The programmes for the games at home against Falkirk and Celtic on 1 and 4 September respectively. The 'Bairns' were beaten 4-1 in midweek and the 'Bhoys' 3-2 on the Saturday as Hearts won their section ahead of Dundee by two points. The quarter-final draw was kind to Hearts as they were drawn against St Johnstone from the lower 'B' Division.

HEART of MIDLOTHIAN
FOOTBALL CLUB LTD.
OFFICIAL PROGRAMME

SCOTTISH LEAGUE CUP

Photo by Scottish Daily Mail

HEART OF MIDLOTHIAN 4
v. FALKIRK

Price
3D

Vol. IX. No. 4.   WEDNESDAY, 1st SEPTEMBER 1954.

HEART of MIDLOTHIAN
FOOTBALL CLUB LTD.
OFFICIAL PROGRAMME

SCOTTISH LEAGUE CUP

HEART OF MIDLOTHIAN
v. CELTIC

Price
3D

Vol. IX. No. 5.   SATURDAY, 4th SEPTEMBER 1954.

Above: Both programmes for the quarter-final League Cup ties against St Johnstone. Hearts won the first leg at Muirton Park 5-0 on 22 September and 2-0 in the return game on 25 September 1954.

Left: The semi-final programme for Hearts *v*. Airdrie, played at Easter Road.

and another when Parker won the toss. Another cheer in the first minute. Mackenzie booted the ball down the middle. It was too far ahead and too fast for Bauld but Fir Park keeper Hastie Weir put panic in the Motherwell breasts by dropping it. But he recovered again in the nick of time. Hearts were going all out from the beginning. Bauld blasted in a shot from the left, then McSeveney, making his first-team debut for Motherwell, had to clear lustily from Souness. Hearts got a wee Hampden roar for their foraging work. Urquhart made progress next and Kilmarnock could only head over for a corner, a fruitless one unfortunately. It was all Hearts for 7 minutes. But then Motherwell broke away. Ex-Hearts wing half Charlie Cox pushed a nice shot through to Bain and the centre took advantage of a Glidden slide on the wet ground to race through the middle. The young centre from Cockenzie Star kicked a powerful drive. Duff was beaten but the shot went over. That wet ground proved a real tragedy for Motherwell in 9 minutes. Conn passed through on the right to Souness. Jim was obviously intending to put a straight pass into the middle of the field when centre half Paton slipped, and as he went down the right-winger saw his chance and rushed forward before parting. It was a beautiful cross and there was Willie Bauld to head the ball into the net away from Weir. Hearts' football was first class keeping the ball on the ground, moving sweetly, and passing from wing to wing. They had the Motherwell defence worried often. Yet it was not all one way. The Fir Parkers broke through on the right and a nice cross shot found ex-Heart Archie Williams in position. His header though gave Duff no trouble. It went high over the bar. In 16 minutes Hearts were two ahead and the glorious Bauld scored this one too. It was a right-wing move which found Conn pushing the ball into the middle again. Bauld got it, switched it from one foot to the other and shook off the attentions of two defenders. He chose his time and placed the ball beautifully into the net. The Hearts fans were in ecstasies. Then Hearts, cheered on by a miniature Hampden Roar, were on the warpath again. Wardhaugh chased a long ball to the corner flag then crossed. The Motherwell defence was in a fankle, Weir pushed it out, Urquhart knocked it in again and the goal was only saved through a goal-line clearance by Cox. The excitement was tense. Then came that dreadful moment that has haunted Hearts in several games this season. The dreaded penalty award. Conn upended Humphries inside the box and Redpath scored in 28 minutes. This was the testing period for Hearts. Was there to be the defensive panic? It looked like it for Hunter broke away on the right and it took a long run by goalkeeper Duff out to the touchline to break up the attack. It was a good game. Hard, exciting, thrilling, worthy of the reputations of both these colourful teams. Then, with the interval whistle almost on us Hearts made further ground. Souness crossed into the middle a high ball and Wardhaugh literally flew at it to head a great third goal.

Half time: Hearts 3 – Motherwell 1.

This was Duff's first Cup Final in his first season in Hearts' first team. On his display so far he earned a first prize. Now Hearts were off again. Mackenzie pushed through a perfect pass up the middle. Bauld beat Paton as he had done all afternoon. Clean through, Willie collided with the advancing Hastie Weir and fell flat. The centre required attention before limping away. Parker and Mackay were egging Hearts on. The skipper was tremendous setting off attacks as well as stemming them. Yet the balance of play was in favour of Motherwell now. There was no relaxing in the pace. It was red-hot stuff. It sizzled and it had the fans on their toes all the time. Rain? That was forgotten. It was obvious that the edge had gone from the Hearts attack. I lay the blame for that on the injury to Bauld. It was seen that he was not so fast, not so aggressive and Paton was finding it easier to hold him. With about 10 minutes to go Motherwell were still fighting grimly. Hearts? Still defending grimly. With four minutes to go the Tynecastle followers were already beginning to sing their victory song. Then what a storming finish. With less than three minutes to go, we had a couple of goals. Fortunately they were divided and it was the injured Bauld who scored from a header from a Wardhaugh pass to get his hat-trick in 87 minutes. Motherwell's reply was sharp. Down they stepped and Bain in less than a minute got his foot to the ball to prod it home.

Final result: Hearts 4 – Motherwell 2

At the final whistle there were astonishing scenes as hundreds of Hearts fans ran onto the pitch to congratulate their heroes as the City of Glasgow Police tried in vain to hold them back. After the game the respective managers met with a smile in the corridor outside the dressing rooms. The Motherwell manager, George Stevenson, extended his hand to the self-effacing Tommy Walker and in true sporting fashion said, 'We must always be disappointed in reverse but all of us at Fir Park congratulate you, Tommy, on your victory. What regrets we may have are softened by the manner in which our boys fought.' And with that Stevenson walked away quietly to leave Walker and his players to celebrate. There is always something so sad, so forlorn about a beaten team. Sympathy but no glory, and in the past Heart of Midlothian had had plenty experience of that. But now it was back to Edinburgh on the team bus to meet the thousands waiting for them. This time it was different, this time Hearts had a trophy to take back to 'Auld Reekie' to show their fans.

The following was penned by 'MacNib' in praise of Willie Bauld.

The Bank Rate may gang soaran up,
Dear milk may fill our bitter cup,
The weather may be dreich and cauld,
But never mind--- we've Willie Bauld.
Hibs in the cup gaed doon the drain,
They still hang murderers in Spain,
Bairns eat us oot o' hoose and hauld,
But never mind--- we've Willie Bauld.
Hire purchase traders get the dunt,
There's trouble on the TV front,
The hail dang system needs owerhauled,
But things leuk up – we've Willie Bauld.
There's some of us are past our best,
We dinna face the spring wi zest,
But there are comforts when ye're auld,
And ane o' them is Willie Bauld.

Team captain Bobby Parker, Tommy Walker and John Harvey with the League Cup.

Jimmy Wardhaugh, middle row second from right, pictured at Hampden Park in the 1970s with sports journalist colleagues. In the front row, third and fourth from the right, are none other than the legendary Jim 'Scoop' Rodger and James Sanderson. Wardhaugh's competitive debut was against Celtic in a League game at Tynecastle on 21 August 1946 at the age of 17 and scored his first goal for Hearts in a 3-2 victory. In 518 appearances he scored 376 goals, a quite incredible feat. Jimmy joined Dunfermline in November 1959 but he remained Hearts' top League goalscorer until May 1997 when John Robertson broke the record in a 3-1 defeat of Rangers at Tynecastle. The fans affectionately called Willie 'Twinkletoes' because of his deft footwork and goal-scoring abilities but for some strange reason he only received two caps for Scotland during his playing career. When his playing days were over Jimmy became a sports journalist with the *Scottish Daily Express*. Jimmy Wardhaugh died on 2 January 1978 after returning home from reporting on an East Fife *v*. Hearts game. He was 48 years of age.

Willie Bauld heads past Motherwell's Hastie Weir for the opening goal. Alongside him are his striking partners Wardhaugh and Conn. Charlie Cox, on the ground, and Willie Kilmarnock are the two other Motherwell players in the photograph.

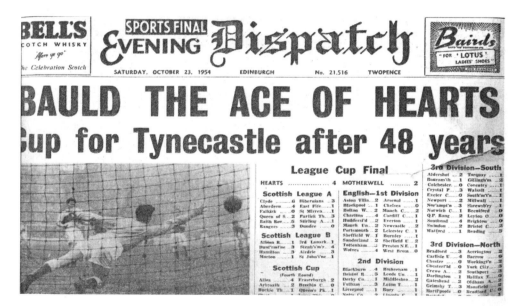

Headlines from the front page of the *Edinburgh Evening Dispatch* of 23 October 1954. The *Evening Dispatch* was a favourite of all fans in Edinburgh and the surrounding areas and was sold on the streets on Saturday nights and at newsagents which had remained open later than normal. It covered virtually all sports and also reported on not just senior football but football played at all levels. The other evening newspaper available was the *Edinburgh Evening News*, the 'Pink', which more or less provided the same coverage but invariably most people bought both to be read from front to back. In 1963 the *Dispatch* was bought over by the *Scotsman* and consequently merged with the *Evening News*, leaving the 'Pink' to give exclusive coverage to sport in Edinburgh. Time also caught up with this version of the famous old newspaper and sadly 2002 saw the last edition being printed as modern technology took over.

Right: Ecstatic scenes in Scotland's capital as the team bus inches its way slowly through the crowds of cheering fans who had waited patiently for the return of their heroes from Hampden. The celebrations continued well into the 'wee sma' oors'.

Below: Wardhaugh holds the trophy with left to right: Blackwood, Mackay, Bauld, Mackenzie, Duff, Conn, Glidden and Cumming.

Above: A souvenir pennant for the League Cup final.

Left: The programme for the 1954/55 League Cup final. A little-known fact about this game was that three players taking part had all played as schoolboys for the same village team. Alfie Conn, Freddie Glidden and Willie Redpath all played for Stoneyburn Public School in the 1940s.

Above: During the 1950s and 60s, a regular feature in the match programme was a series of cartoons by the artist Ian White which was named the 'Gorgie Giggles', as seen in this publication.

Right: Programme for the Hearts *v.* Aberdeen Scottish Cup tie.

THE LEAGUE CHAMPIONSHIP

Hearts collected full points from their opening two fixtures, with wins against Partick Thistle and Hibs, but then suffered a 3-2 defeat at Dens Park. However they got back on the winning trail by beating East Fife away from home before the League Cup final. After the euphoria of the Cup win it was back to League business once again and two good wins against Stirling Albion and Falkirk kept the 'feel good' factor going among the support, but a series of indifferent results saw the side finish in fourth place by the end of the season. But two notable results kept the fans happy – League and Cup wins over Hibernian. On New Year's Day 1955, Hibernian first-footed their Edinburgh neighbours only to find that Hearts were not in a neighbourly mood as they inflicted a 5-1 defeat on the men from Leith in front of 49,000 spectators.

THE SCOTTISH CUP

Five weeks later, Hibernian returned to Gorgie in the second round of the Scottish Cup with some trepidation, which as it turned out was well founded. 'The Terrible Trio' terrorised the Hibs defence, scoring all five goals between them. In the next round Hearts disposed of Buckie Thistle 6-0 in the Highlands and were given a home draw against Aberdeen for their efforts. A 1-1 draw between the sides on 5 March took Hearts to Pittodrie in midweek for the replay. Alas they went down 2-0 to a strong Aberdeen side who went on to win the League Championship that season. Although disappointed, the support reflected on the season, which saw the emergence of Dave Mackay, and they looked forward to the following one with a lot of optimism.

SEASON 1955/56

This would be the season that would see the Scottish Cup return to Tynecastle after an absence of fifty years and Hearts finish in third place in the League. In the League Cup, Aberdeen, the eventual winners, would put out the holders in the quarter-finals.

THE LEAGUE CUP

An excellent start to the campaign saw Hearts win five of their six sectional games, scoring 15 goals in the process for the loss of two and finishing top of the group. Their only defeat was at Methil, where they went down 1-0 to East Fife. The quarter-finals saw them paired with Aberdeen. The first leg at Pittodrie on 14 September was won by the 'Dons' 5-3 and three days later it was a case of 'job done' with a 4-2 victory in Edinburgh. Defeat was no disgrace as Aberdeen were an excellent team at that time and would go on to win the trophy by defeating St Mirren 2-1 in the final the following month.

THE LEAGUE CHAMPIONSHIP

The League campaign got off to a good start with the 4-0 defeat of Dundee. However, following a 1-0 defeat by Hibs at Tynecastle, in the next seven games only four wins were recorded and the mood of the support wasn't helped by having to suffer a 4-1 trouncing by Rangers at Ibrox. Nonetheless there was a bit of light at the end of the tunnel in the shape of Johnny Hamilton, Ian Crawford and Alex Young as these three began to make their mark in the team. The eighteen-year-old Young in particular would later come to be idolised by the fans and was known as the 'Golden Vision'. Hearts then began to put a run of good results together and going into the festive period they were in second place with twenty-one points. Celtic were the leaders on twenty-three points, but Hearts had played a game less. However, lurking behind them in third spot with twenty points were Rangers, who had a game in hand over Hearts and two in hand over Celtic. In fourth place, also with twenty points, were Hibernian. So expectations were on a high as the team travelled across

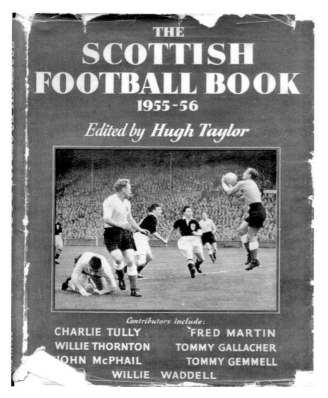

Above left: The Scottish Football Book 1955/56.

Above right: Programme for Hearts' League Cup quarter-final tie with Aberdeen. The front cover for the programme saw another change, with an eye-catching candy stripe surrounding an action photograph. It was still a twelve-page issue.

to Fife on Hogmanay to take on Raith Rovers at Stark's Park. The game finished 1-1 and then the news filtered through that Celtic, Rangers and Hibs had all recorded victories. Two days later, more agony was to follow as Hearts dropped another vital point in a 2-2 draw at Easter Road. Meanwhile, along the road in Glasgow the Old Firm encounter saw Rangers triumph 1-0, putting them in second place. The next week Celtic suffered another defeat as Rangers went top courtesy of a 3-1 win over Dundee. The Ibrox club would remain there till the end of the season. Hearts continued to hang on to Rangers' coat-tails but defeats away from home to Partick Thistle and Aberdeen in April effectively put paid to their Championship aspirations and they finished in third place.

THE SCOTTISH CUP

The road to Hampden began with a 3-0 defeat of Forfar Athletic on 4 February at Tynecastle, with Conn bagging a brace and Hamilton the other. The next round

Above left: Programme for Hearts' Scottish Cup fifth round tie against Forfar Athletic.

Above right: Programme for Hearts' tie against Stirling Albion.

was another favourable draw, this time a home game against Stirling Albion. The 'Trio' all scored along, with John Cumming and Alex Young, in a 5-0 rout as Hearts marched into the quarter-finals. In the 'hat' for the next round were Airdrie, Celtic, Clyde, Partick Thistle, Rangers, Raith Rovers and the romantically named Queen of the South. Every ear in Gorgie was pressed to every available radio as the draw was made. First out were Celtic with a home tie against Airdrie. Next were Hearts. 'Great, we're at home,' shouted the support in unison. The tension was unbearable as they waited to hear who their opponents would be... 'Versus Rangers.' 'Aw naw, no thaim,' exclaimed the fans. It was the draw the Hearts fans didn't want and you could understand why. In the previous rounds Rangers had beaten Aberdeen and Dundee and were unbeaten in the league in fifteen games stretching back to October. But Hearts had also put together an impressive run in the League, their last defeat being the 4-1 defeat at Ibrox in November. Nonetheless the bookies had already installed Rangers as favourites to lift the trophy, but Tommy Walker's philosophy was simple. He knew that to win the Cup you had to meet the favourites at some point, so why not now. So the stage was set for what was undoubtedly the game of the day.

Above left: The programme for the seventh round tie against Rangers.

Above right: Houston, the Stirling Albion goalkeeper, punches clear from Willie Bauld in the Cup game on 18 February at Tynecastle.

Both teams came out to a thunderous roar from the 47,258 within the stadium. The team line-ups were:

Hearts: Duff, Kirk, Mackenzie, Mackay, Glidden, Cumming, Young, Conn, Bauld, Wardhaugh, Crawford.

Rangers: Niven, Shearer, Little, McColl, Young, Rae, Scott, Simpson, Kichenbrand, Baird, Hubbard.

Apart from the Main Stand and enclosure, the game was not all-ticket as Edinburgh City Police deemed that it wasn't necessary, and quite a few eyebrows were raised at this decision. Tynecastle's capacity back then was 49,000 but the police were confident that their decision was the correct one and as it transpired 47,258 fans clicked through the turnstiles. The early stages of the game were totally dominated by the Glasgow side as they forced corner after corner, but they couldn't capitalise on their early pressure and gradually Hearts began to take control, with Cumming and Mackay stamping their authority on proceedings. In 37 minutes Hearts took the lead when Ian Crawford headed home. Rangers were still trying to recover from that blow when a minute later Bauld scored a second. Tynecastle was rockin' – Rangers were reelin'. But the Hearts support had long memories of disappointments and tried not to get too carried away during the half-time break. Despite being two goals down, they knew Rangers would come out fighting for the second half. That's exactly what happened but the Hearts defence, marshalled by Glidden, stood firm and then with 25 minutes remaining Alfie Conn fired a powerful drive from about eighteen yards past Niven to put the game beyond Rangers. In 72 minutes you could almost hear Willie Bauld quoting an old Scots phrase, 'I'll mak' siccar' (I'll make sure), as he ran in to score the fourth. There were warm handshakes all round at the final whistle between the sides as they left the field. The Scottish press then mused that perhaps the body blow that Rangers had received would have an adverse effect on their title challenge and maybe Hearts could take advantage. That thought was quickly dispelled four days later as Rangers beat Queen of the South 8-0 at Ibrox in what was the first ever Scottish League game played under floodlights.

The draw for the semi-finals of the Cup paired Celtic against Clyde and Hearts against Raith Rovers. Easter Road was the chosen venue for the Gorgie outfit where they would meet the men from Fife on Saturday 24 March. The game was played in front of 58,488 and finished 0-0, although both sides had chances throughout the match. The replay took place four days later with another massive turnout of 54,233 inside Easter Road. In the very first minute of the game Jimmy Wardhaugh gave the Maroons the lead and they never looked back. Wardhaugh scored a second and with a few minutes remaining, a cross by Johnny Hamilton was met by the head of Ian Crawford to make the final result Hearts 3 Raith Rovers 0. In the other semi-final Celtic had already disposed of Clyde. The date for the final was set for Saturday 21 April.

The semi-final programme for Hearts *v.* Raith Rovers at Easter Road. The programme notes highlighted the forthcoming Cup final plans, which would be all-ticket, and listed the pricing for the various parts of the ground along with the ticket distribution. It made interesting reading:

Stands – 21 shillings; 10 shillings and sixpence; 7 shillings and sixpence and 5 shillings.
Enclosures – 3 shillings and sixpence.
Terraces – 2 shillings and sixpence.
Boys' Enclosure – 1 shilling and sixpence.

   The competing clubs are entitled to 20 per cent of tickets at all prices. This means that each of the finalists can claim about 27,000 tickets, a figure based on a Hampden limit of 135,000. After the finalists, official bodies and travel agencies are given quotas, the remainder of the tickets will be on sale to the general public.

Niven holds a shot while Rae offers protection from the onrushing Conn in the Scottish Cup game on 3 March 1956. Alfie Conn joined Hearts in June 1944 and made his competitive debut in a Southern League match against Dumbarton in October of that year. In comparison to Wardhaugh and Bauld he was small in height but Alfie more than made up for this with a great upper-body physique and this, coupled with his sheer aggression, made a fearsome opponent. Injuries curtailed his appearances for Hearts in latter seasons but he still managed to play 408 games for the side, 339 of them being competitive fixtures. He last wore the Number 8 jersey for the Maroons in a 4-0 defeat of Aberdeen at home on 16 April 1958. In September 1958 Alfie was transferred to Raith Rovers for a fee of £2,250 and the curtain came down on the 'Terrible Trio' for the final time. Note the black armbands worn by the players in the photograph. This was in a mark of respect to Mr William MacAndrew of the Scottish Football League, who had died the night before the game.

Opposite above: Willie Duff clears from Rangers centre forward Kichenbrand in the second half of the match while Tam Mackenzie and Freddie Glidden look on.

Joining Hearts during the Second World War years, 'Big Tam' made his competitive debut in the Hearts colours against Clyde in 1942. His tackling of opponents was superb but he had other qualities, namely his passing of the ball. He made 421 appearances for Hearts, of which 359 were competitive games. Tom's final competitive game was on 23 November 1957 against Clyde and the Hearts support saw for the last time the great partnership of Parker and Mackenzie, who had served the club with distinction for many years.

Dave Mackay and Freddie Glidden in an
aerial duel with Don Kichenbrand of Rangers.

Although born in Lanarkshire, Freddie
Glidden's formative years were spent in
the West Lothian mining village of Bents,
Stoneyburn and coincidentally he lived on
the same street as Alfie Conn. He began his
footballing days by playing for Stoneyburn
Public School, as did Conn. Who would have
thought that all those years later both would
appear together for Hearts in two major
cup finals? Freddie provisionally signed for
Hearts in July 1945 and was loaned out
to Newtongrange Star. On his return to
Tynecastle he made his competitive debut
on 10 November 1951 against Queen of the
South. Glidden played in various positions
in defence before settling into the centre half
berth and making that position virtually his
own before eventually being displaced by
Jimmy Milne. Freddie Glidden played a total
of 270 games including friendlies and his last
appearance was in a League game at Rugby
Park, Kilmarnock on 29 November 1958. He
joined Dumbarton in 1959 before finishing
his career in 1962.

Willie Duff gathers the ball, watched by Don Kichenbrand, Dave Mackay, Bobby Kirk and Freddie Glidden.

Glidden sees the ball out with Kichenbrand once again in attendance.

Glidden heads away from Kichenbrand as Wardhaugh, Cumming and Mackay stand by.
Also in the photo are Billy Simpson and Johnny Hubbard of Rangers.

Willie Bauld looks on as Alex Young wins this heading duel with Willie Rae of Rangers
while Johnny Little, Rangers' number three, attempts to bring the ball under control.

Jimmy Wardhaugh shakes hands
with Rangers' George Niven
after the 4-0 victory.

CUP FINAL DAY

As expected, there was great excitement in Scotland's capital city as Hearts prepared
for their visit to Hampden Park on Saturday 21 April 1956. The exact figure of
Hearts supporters who travelled through to Glasgow for the game varies but it was
thought to be in the region of 50,000. Hearts played Falkirk on the Monday before
the final and had beaten the 'Bairns' 8-3, so confidence was high in the Tynecastle
camp. By contrast Celtic's League form had been up and down, with their line-ups
changing from game to game. For the final Celtic were without Jock Stein and the
influential Bobby Collins, both of whom had been out injured for several weeks.
The major talking point of the game arrived 45 minutes before kick-off when the
team news was announced. The Celtic support were stunned with unexpected team
changes which saw several players being played out of position and most certainly,
in the eyes of the Parkhead fans, handing their opponents the advantage. But games
aren't won on paper and Hearts knew all about Celtic's fighting spirit, more so in
Cup games. For their part Hearts were unchanged from the side which had beaten
Falkirk earlier in the week. A point to note from the game was that five players
taking part had all previously played for the Midlothian junior side Newtongrange
Star: Bauld, Glidden, Mackay and Young and Haughney of Celtic.

The team line-ups were:

Celtic: Beattie, Meechan, Fallon, Smith, Evans, Peacock, Craig, Haughney, Mochan, Fernie, Tully.

Hearts: Duff, Kirk, Mackenzie, Mackay, Glidden, Cumming. Young, Conn, Bauld, Wardhaugh, Crawford.

The following is a report of the game from Saturday night's *Edinburgh Evening Dispatch*, as reported by Bill Heeps.

Freddie Glidden got Hearts off to a good start by winning the toss and taking advantage of the strong wind. Celtic kicked off against the breeze, but were quickly turned about by Mackay. Fallon obstructed Young in Hearts' first attack but Kirk's free-kick was headed over by Bauld from a difficult angle. There was an anxious moment for Hearts when the ball bounced away from Mackenzie and left Craig in the clear but the raid petered out. Both teams were taking time to settle and the play was rather scrappy at the start. Crawford, playing well on the left, was fouled by Meechan but Cumming's kick was confidently cleared by Evans. Tame mid-field play kept the vast crowd subdued. Neither team could really get on top. Suddenly the scene changed in 17 minutes when Wardhaugh stroked a perfect pass to Crawford. The winger took time to shoot from an angle but Beattie stuck out a foot and the ball swirled away for a fruitless corner. Hearts were beginning to show their teeth now and the terracing was aflame with maroon when they took the lead in 20 minutes. It was a snap shot by Crawford which did the trick. Beattie obviously anticipated a cross from the winger after he was put through by Conn. It was fitting that Crawford should have scored for he was Hearts' most progressive forward. There was no denying Hearts' superiority now as they had the Celtic goal under constant siege. The best reply Celtic could muster was a breakaway raid which ended with Mochan heading past a Craig cross. Celtic got a corner seconds

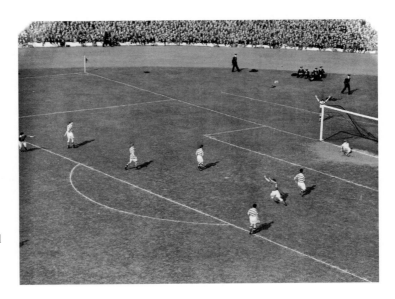

Ian Crawford, seen here on the extreme left, scoring the first of his two goals in the Scottish Cup final as Alfie Conn runs over to congratulate him.

The Celtic goalkeeper, Dick Beattie, is helpless as Crawford's shot hits the net to put Hearts one up. Ian Crawford arrived at Tynecastle via Hibernian and Hamilton Academical at the beginning of the 1954/55 campaign, making his debut against Motherwell at Fir Park on 18 April of that season. He played mainly in the outside left position and had tremendous pace when running at opposition defences. Ian made 174 competitive first-team appearances for Hearts, playing his last game on 29 March 1961 in an East of Scotland Shield tie against Hibernian. He was transferred to West Ham a few months later for a fee in the region of £7,000.

Crawford fires in another shot, which Beattie saves.

later but Haughney headed over. Celtic were beginning to hit back now and their forwards were controlling the ball against the wind. Hearts had held the initiative in the first half but the attack hadn't quite clicked into their best form. Young had been more or less starved of the ball and Bauld found it difficult to make progress against Evans. It would have been more comforting for Hearts if they had built up a more commanding lead while they had the wind behind them but their along-the-ground football would perhaps stand them in good stead in the second-half. Seconds before the interval there was further worry for Hearts when Cumming had to be assisted from the field with a gashed brow. He had been hurt in a collision with Fernie. After treatment Fernie was able to carry on.

Half time: Celtic 0 – Hearts 1

There were two cheers for Hearts when play resumed, one for the team and one for John Cumming who had a plaster over his forehead. Disaster almost overtook Hearts in a matter of seconds when the ball was jammed between Craig and Mackenzie. It eluded Duff as he left his goal but the Parkhead winger shot weakly past. Hearts' vision of the Scottish Cup on the Tynecastle sideboard became clearer than ever when young Crawford scored a beautiful second goal. Bauld was the architect. He trailed the ball for forty yards up the wing as Crawford cleverly took over the vacant spot left in the middle. After tricking Evans, Bauld sent over a perfect cross. Alex Young headed it down to the feet of Crawford who hit it cleanly into the net. Hearts' jubilation was somewhat curbed however in 53 minutes when Haughney reduced the leeway. Tully was impeded but his free-kick was held by Duff. Haughney charged Duff, who dropped the ball and the full-back turned forward prodded it into the net. But Hearts did not allow the goal to upset them and they forced three corners. Bauld had a chance but he failed to connect with a pass from Crawford. Cumming was a stalwart in defence but had lost his plaster. He carried a sponge to wipe away the blood which flowed freely from the wound on his head. It would be a tragedy if such gallantry was not rewarded. He got another hard knock but carried on with grim determination. After 20 odd minutes Celtic changed their attack and the atmosphere was tense as time ran out. In 80 minutes Conn sealed a fighting Hearts win when he scored from fifteen yards. A Bauld header broke to the inside right who steadied himself before hammering the ball into the net off the hands of the despairing Beattie.

Full time result: Celtic 1 – Hearts 3.

Attendance: 132,840.

Crawford scores the second goal to make it Hearts 2 Celtic 0.

The second goal photographed from behind the goals.

Number eight, Alfie Conn, wheels away after making the score Hearts 3 Celtic 1 in the 80th minute.

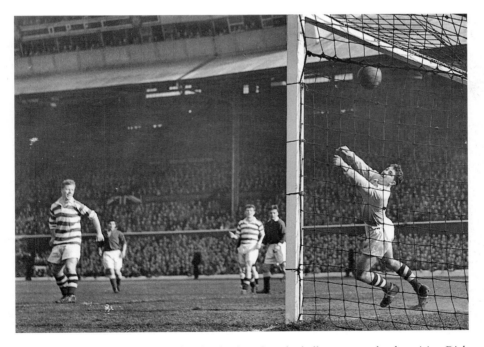

Conn's shot about to hit the net for the third goal as the ball goes past the despairing Dick Beattie. Bobby Evans and Frank Meechan are the Celtic players, along with Ian Crawford and Willie Bauld.

From left to right, Duff, Mackenzie, Mackay, Wardhaugh and Cumming can only look on as Haughney scores Celtic's goal.

Willie Duff drops the ball after a shoulder charge by Haughney, who prods the ball home in this picture of Celtic's goal taken from behind the goal line.

Action from the Cup final sees Bobby Kirk and Willie Fernie in a tussle for the ball. Bobby joined Hearts from Raith Rovers in May 1955 and made his competitive debut on 13 August that year, the day after his twenty-eighth birthday. He quickly settled into the side and could play in either of the full-back positions. Steadfast and reliable, Bobby was a quiet and unassuming person and a much valued member of the team. He was one of those players who got on with the task in hand with the minimum of fuss and was a role model for his younger colleagues. In season 1959/60 he played in every League and Cup game for Hearts, a remarkable achievement. In April 1963 he was given a free transfer by Hearts but only learned this by way of the newspapers, which hurt him deeply. Bobby Kirk made 292 competitive appearances for Hearts, scoring 12 goals, all from penalties, and he won every major honour in Scottish football while at Tynecastle.

John Cumming is helped off by John Harvey and Donald McLeod to receive treatment after a collision with Celtic's Willie Fernie just before half-time. In the background players from both sides gather round the injured Fernie, seen lying on the ground.

The final whistle sees the Hearts players going off the field to receive their winners' medals as the disconsolate Celtic team look on.

Above: The team bus making its way past the Tynecastle Arms public house in Gorgie Road at the junction with McLeod Street.

Amazing scenes of jubilation as the Edinburgh City Police motorcyclist and mounted branches attempt to create a 'corridor' for the Hearts official party as they make their way to the Charlotte Rooms in Charlotte Street for the celebration dinner.

The open-top double-decker bus supplied by the SMT bus company, suitably logoed with 'Hearts Are Trumps', with players and officials on the top deck. At the front two-goal hero Ian Crawford is seen holding the Cup, flanked on his right by Freddie Glidden and John Cumming, with Jimmy Wardhaugh on the left.

John Cumming, complete with plaster, takes a well-earned drink from the Cup as a beaming Alfie Conn looks on.

John Cumming was signed on provisional forms by Hearts in 1948 while playing for his local junior team, Carluke Rovers, before arriving in Gorgie in January 1950. John made his debut in a League game against Celtic on 30 December of that year in a 2-2 draw at Celtic Park. He played in the outside left position initially but then moved to the left-half position in midfield. Cumming was known as the 'Iron Man', a name bestowed on him by sports journalists because of his fighting spirit and 'never say die' attitude. In 612 first-team appearances in a maroon jersey he was never booked by a referee, which said it all about the man. John played his last competitive first-team game for Hearts on 12 November 1966 against Dunfermline and retired from playing at the end of that season. He went on to serve the club in the capacity of trainer/physio until 1976. John Cumming was a loyal and faithful servant to Heart of Midlothian and will always be remembered by the fans and be part of their folklore.

Above left: The programme for the 1955/56 Scottish Cup final.

Above right: The souvenir programme issued for the last home game, against Raith Rovers on 28 April 1956, with the front cover showing the players proudly holding the trophy.

The League game against Hibs at Tynecastle on 24 September 1955 sees Hibs 'keeper Tommy Younger holding a shot with Willie McFarlane on the line. The Hearts players are Souness, Blackwood, Young and Wardhaugh.

Jimmy Souness joined Hearts from Hibs in January 1953 after six years at Easter Road and made his debut against Partick Thistle at Firhill the same month. He proved to be an excellent acquisition for the Maroons and was prominent in the games leading up to the League Cup win in season 1954/55. Jimmy was noted for his speed in the outside right berth and scored many solo goals in his time at Tynecastle. After three years at the club he was released from his contract to work full-time as an actuary with an insurance company.

Tommy Younger and Bobby Combe of Hibernian with Alex Young. Hibs won this Edinburgh derby 1-0, the goal, scored by Jimmy Mulkerrin, coming five minutes from the end.

Jimmy Souness heads over the bar after a mistake in the air by Tommy Younger. John Paterson of Hibs is on the goal line. Other players in the photograph are Bobby Blackwood. Alfie Conn and Jimmy Wardhaugh.

Alex Young, Jimmy Wardhaugh and Johnny Urquhart in action against East Fife in October 1955. Johnny Urquhart joined Hearts in August 1944, making his competitive debut in October against Dumbarton in a Southern League fixture. It wasn't until 1951/52 season that he began to string first-team appearances together, mainly on the left wing. He was virtually a constant in the side for the next four seasons and was instrumental in the League Cup final defeat of Motherwell. Johnny eventually lost his place in the team to Ian Crawford and played his last game for Hearts in a League fixture against Partick Thistle on 2 April 1956 before being transferred to Raith Rovers.

Alex Young puts the ball past Freddie Martin for his first goal in a League game at Tynecastle on 3 December 1955.

Martin gathers safely from Bauld as Clunie and Caldwell of Aberdeen look on.

Jimmy Whittle, lying on the ground, gives Hearts the lead against Airdrie, 21 January 1956.

Action from the same game
sees the Airdrie goalkeeper,
Walker, scramble the ball away.

Knocking Reekie

Auld Reekie, when the cup came here,
Revealed a zest long hidden,
When thousands lined the streets to cheer,
The trophy held by Glidden.
Some folk are jealous of our fame,
And dearly love to knock us,
They say we're snobs – what's in a name?
Sour grapes have made them mock us.
Because we have a certain air,
And boost our city's beauty,
Our poor relations all declare,
We're far to blooming snooty.
But still our city stands supreme,
In all this dearly bought land,
Of Caledonia the cream,
The Cup-ital of Scotland.

The above was penned by 'MacNib' and appeared in the *Edinburgh Evening
Dispatch* newspaper following the Cup win over Celtic.

SEASON 1956/57

It would be a season when Hearts would fail to qualify for the final stages of the League Cup, crash out of the Scottish Cup and be involved in a dramatic finish to the League Championship as they and Rangers fought it out for supremacy in Scotland.

THE LEAGUE CUP

The season got underway with the Tynecastle men playing hosts to rivals Hibs on 11 August in the opening League Cup fixture. Also in the four-team section were Falkirk and Partick Thistle. The Hearts support couldn't have asked for a better start as their favourites took Hibs apart in a 6-1 mauling despite going behind to an Eddie Turnbull goal. But the joy was short-lived as a midweek trip to Maryhill brought a 3-1 defeat at the hands of Partick Thistle. This defeat was to prove costly as Hearts finished in second place in their section to the Glasgow side affectionately known as the 'Maryhill Magyars'.

THE LEAGUE CHAMPIONSHIP

The League Championship began with a hard-earned 3-2 victory over Dunfermline in Fife but there was a wee bit of inconsistency in their form, not helped by an injury to Conn which would see him out till January. After a 5-2 defeat by East Fife at home the side began to click, putting some very impressive results together, including a 3-2 defeat at home of nearest challengers Motherwell on 8 December. This result put them clear of the 'Steelmen' by five points at the top of the League. The following game against Rangers at Ibrox was a vital one in terms of winning the Championship. The Gers had just been thumped 5-1 at Starks Park by Raith Rovers and were in fourth place, seven points behind Hearts, although they had two games in hand over the men from the capital. Hearts arrived in Govan in a confident frame of mind, borne out by their recent performances. The match programme notes spoke of Hearts in glowing terms:

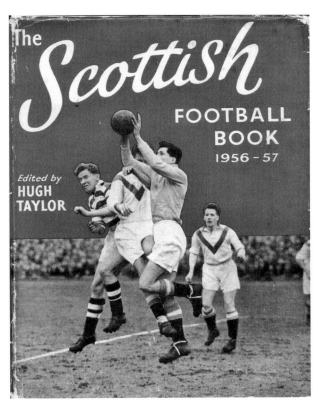

The Scottish Football Book 1956/57.

Tynecastle, 17 November 1956. Former Hearts 'keeper Jimmy Brown punches clear from Jimmy Wardhaugh and Alex Young in a League game which Hearts won 3-2. Also in the photograph are Hearts' Jim McFadzean, with Matt Watson and Willie Toner of Kilmarnock.

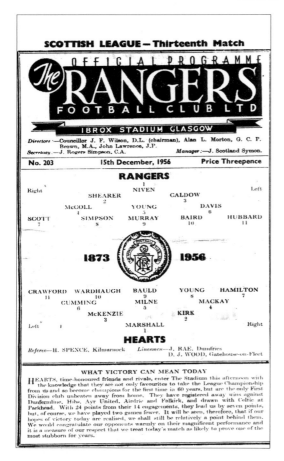

OFFICIAL PROGRAMME

The RANGERS
FOOTBALL CLUB LTD

IBROX STADIUM GLASGOW

Directors :—Councillor J. F. Wilson, D.L. (chairman), Alan L. Morton, G. C. P. Brown, M.A., John Lawrence, J.P.
Secretary :—J. Rogers Simpson, C.A.   *Manager :*—J. Scotland Symon.

| No. 203 | 15th December, 1956 | Price Threepence |

RANGERS

NIVEN
1

Right   SHEARER   CALDOW   Left
2   3

McCOLL   YOUNG   DAVIS
4   5   6

SCOTT   SIMPSON   MURRAY   BAIRD   HUBBARD
7   8   9   10   11

1873   1956

CRAWFORD   WARDHAUGH   BAULD   YOUNG   HAMILTON
11   10   9   8   7

CUMMING   MILNE   MACKAY
6   5   4

McKENZIE   KIRK
3   2

Left   1   MARSHALL   Right
1

HEARTS

Referee—H. SPENCE, Kilmarnock   *Linesmen*—J. RAE, Dumfries
D. J. WOOD, Gatehouse-on-Fleet

WHAT VICTORY CAN MEAN TODAY

HEARTS, time-honoured friends and rivals, enter The Stadium this afternoon with the knowledge that they are not only favourites to take the League Championship from us and so become champions for the first time in 60 years, but are the only First Division club unbeaten away from home. They have registered away wins against Dunfermline, Hibs, Ayr United, Airdrie and Falkirk, and drawn with Celtic at Parkhead. With 24 points from their 14 engagements, they lead us by seven points, but, of course, we have played two games fewer. It will be seen, therefore, that if our hopes of victory today are realised, we shall still be relatively a point behind them. We would congratulate our opponents warmly on their magnificent performance and it is a measure of our respect that we treat today's match as likely to prove one of the most stubborn for years.

Programme for the Scottish League match against Rangers, 15 December 1956.

Hearts, time-honoured friends and rivals enter the stadium this afternoon with the knowledge that they are not only favourites to take the League Championship from us and so becoming champions for the first time in sixty years, but are the only First Division club unbeaten away from home. With 24 points from fourteen engagements, they lead us by 7 points, but, of course, we have played two games fewer. It will be seen therefore, that if our hopes of victory today are realised, we shall still be relatively a point behind them.

It was obvious from the statement that Rangers would not give up the Championship without a fight, and so it proved. In front of a crowd of 45,000 the early honours went to Hearts as they raced into a two-goal lead courtesy of Wardhaugh, who scored in the 16th minute and the 22nd, but Hubbard and Davis scored for Rangers coming up to half-time. In a ten-minute spell in the second period Rangers added three more before Bauld scored a consolation goal with a minute remaining. But the heads didn't go down and the following week the team got back to winning ways by overcoming Queen of the South at home. Meanwhile down in Ayrshire, Kilmarnock were doing Hearts a favour by beating Rangers 3-2. Going into the derby game

Right: The programme for the Hearts *v.* Rangers Scottish Cup tie on 2 February 1957.

Below: Crushing on the terracing during the game caused the crowd to overspill onto the track-side.

Manager Tommy Walker photographed at the rear of the Main Stand at Tynecastle. Signed from Linlithgow Rose in May 1932, Walker made his competitive debut for Hearts on 3 September of the same year and scored in a 4-2 victory over Ayr United. He became an all-time great at Hearts and because of his style of play and all-round ability, Tommy was always attracting interest from teams south of the border. Fan power kept Tommy in Gorgie as the Hearts support always threatened to boycott Tynecastle if their hero was ever transferred. The outbreak of the Second World War interrupted his career but at the age of thirty-one years Tommy was transferred to Chelsea in September 1946. However, after just two years at Stamford Bridge he returned to his first love to assist the then manager, Dave McLean. After the death of Dave McLean in 1951, Tommy took over as manager and thereafter became without question the most successful person ever to occupy the manager's chair in the history of Heart of Midlothian. Tommy Walker was awarded the OBE in November 1960. In 1966, after leading the side to every domestic honour and taking Hearts into Europe, Tommy Walker departed Tynecastle. It was a sad day for the Hearts faithful. He returned in 1974 to join the Hearts Board of Directors before finally retiring in 1980.

A training session at the 'Gorgie End' of the ground sees John Cumming followed by George Thomson, Alex Young, Bobby Blackwood, Jimmy Milne, Jimmy Murray, Jim McFadzean and Willie Bauld leading the rest of the squad.

Alex Parker of Falkirk clears of the line in the 1-1 draw at a snow-covered Tynecastle on 23 February. It was a vital point for the 'Bairns', who were fighting relegation. Not only did Falkirk avoid the 'drop', they went on to win the Scottish Cup in April after beating Kilmarnock 2-1 in a replay.

on Ne'erday against their city rivals, Hearts were still topping the League with a five-point advantage over the 'Light Blues', who still had two games in hand. What better way to start the New Year by defeating the men from Leith and having a party afterwards. Any celebrations the Hearts support had in mind were quickly dashed as their old rivals first-footed them and turned into party poopers by dishing out a 2-0 defeat to the League leaders. Meanwhile, back in Glasgow it was the Rangers fans who were celebrating as they saw their side beat their bitter rivals Celtic 2-0. But Hearts simply picked themselves up, displaying their mettle, and got on with the task in hand: to try and win the League. At the end of January the Maroons were still the leaders as Rangers dropped points in a surprise defeat by Ayr United at Somerset Park.

THE SCOTTISH CUP

The draw for the fifth round of the Scottish Cup saw the holders face Rangers at Tynecastle on 2 February, but history was not repeated as the Glasgow side won 4-0. The game was effectively over by half-time as Rangers led 3-0, with goals from Hubbard, Murray and Scott being scored in a four-minute spell. Simpson added a fourth with ten minutes remaining. It was interesting to note that the Hearts line-up showed only two changes in personnel from the side that had beaten Rangers in the Cup the previous season. Wilson Brown had replaced Willie Duff in goal, with Bobby Parker in for Tam Mackenzie.

Would Hearts' League challenge falter, the critics asked, after the Cup exit at the hands of Rangers? The answer was an emphatic no, as once again manager Tommy Walker rallied his troops and sent them back into the fray. Going into April only four points separated Hearts and Rangers, but the Ibrox men still had those two vital games in hand. The nerves were being shredded. On 13 April Rangers rolled up to Tynecastle to take part in what was going to be a title-decider and the game of the season. The match was decided in the thirty-fifth minute when the Northern Irishman Billy Simpson crashed home a header for the only goal of the game. The Hearts support trudged wearily home that evening, not knowing that exactly a year later they would be hailing their heroes as League Champions. Rangers went on to win their remaining games and snatch the title by two points.

SEASON 1957/58

This was the season when Hearts would win the League Championship for the first time since taking it in 1896/97. Not only would they win the League but they would positively romp it, breaking records in the process. There were disappointments in the League and Scottish Cups, which would go to Celtic and Clyde respectively, but they were quickly forgotten as the League flag returned to fly over Tynecastle for the first time in 61 years. The long wait was over.

THE LEAGUE CUP

Kilmarnock were the opponents in the opening League Cup game on 10 August 1957 and the Hearts support travelled to 'Burns Country' in great numbers, hoping to see the new season get underway with a victory. It was not to be, as Kilmarnock won 2-1. Again this defeat was to prove costly as Hearts finished in second place behind the Ayrshire men in the section. Out of the next five sectional ties they won only two and drew the remainder.

THE LEAGUE CHAMPIONSHIP

Hearts to win the League? 'No chance,' said the experts after the dismal start the Maroons had made to the season. The bookmakers moved quickly once again to install Rangers as favourites to take the title. But one man was confident that Hearts would be Champions, and that was sports journalist Alex Cameron, who in later years became known as 'Candid Cameron' when writing for the *Daily Record*. Alex boldly predicted that the League flag would fly over Tynecastle come the end of the campaign. In the first six League games Hearts were unbeaten, which included a derby win over Hibs at home on 21 September, taking eleven points from a possible twelve.

But the most important game on the calendar was the visit to Ibrox on 26 October to take on Rangers. The previous Saturday, in the final of the League Cup, Rangers had been comprehensively beaten 7-1 by Celtic and manager Tommy Walker warned his men of the dangers of a possible backlash from a hurt and wounded

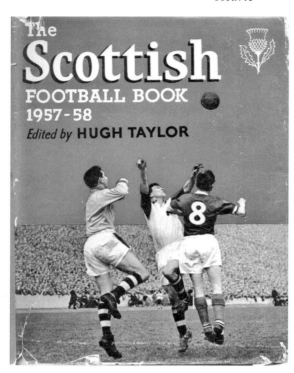

Left: The Scottish Football Book 1957/58.

Below: Heroics from Lawrie Leslie as he parries a header from Jimmy Murray of Hibs in the League game on 21 September 1957.

It's the turn of Gordon Marshall to save as Andy Aitken of Hibs and Hearts centre half Jimmy Milne look on.

Marshall makes another save. Also in the picture, left to right, are Joe Baker, Hibs, Jimmy Milne and Jimmy Murray, with George Thomson on the goal line.

Celtic Park, 28 December 1957, and Celtic's Dick Beattie saves from Alex Young in the League encounter won by Hearts 2-0 with goals from Young and Wardhaugh. Sean Fallon is the other 'Celt' in the photo, with Ian Crawford behind him. Note the covered enclosure in the background. Nicknamed 'The Jungle', it was an intimidating place for visiting teams and fans alike.

side. On a dull and chilly afternoon in Glasgow a crowd of 62,000 saw Rangers race into a two-goal lead as Simpson scored in the 17th and 22nd minutes. Hearts protested vehemently to the referee about the second goal being allowed to stand as their goalkeeper Wilson Brown had quite clearly been fouled by Kichenbrand in the lead up to the goal. But the protests were waved away by referee Bobby Davidson. The Hearts support in the huge crowd saw another defeat in Glasgow looming and another long trek back to Edinburgh beckoned. Their dark mood soon began to change as a Wardhaugh goal just before the interval brought fresh hope. Four minutes into the second half Bauld equalised and suddenly Hearts could taste victory. In the 67th minute Niven, the Rangers goalie, inexplicably let slip from his grasp a shot from Young which ended up in the net to seal a famous win for the Tynecastle outfit. This was the confidence-booster Tommy Walker's side required as they embarked on an amazing run towards securing the League Championship.

Going into the home game against Third Lanark in January, Hearts led the League table by thirteen points over second-placed Rangers, who had four games in hand. The Tynecastle men's only defeat had come at Shawfield on 23 November when a really good Clyde team, lying in third spot in the League, had beaten them 2-1. Clyde would go on to lift the Scottish Cup later on in the season, defeating Hibernian 1-0 in the Hampden final. Since that defeat the Maroons had embarked on a run of ten straight wins but Rangers had also begun to string results together, despite having been knocked out of the European Cup by AC Milan earlier in the season, and would not relinquish the League title without a fight. On 22 February a milestone was passed when Alfie Conn scored Hearts' 100th League goal after a devastating team performance in the 4-0 defeat of Motherwell in North Lanarkshire.

The match programme for the 7-2 victory over Third Lanark, 25 January 1958.

Robert Paton, known as Danny to his friends, is featured on the front cover of the programme. Danny Paton joined Hearts in May 1957 and made his competitive debut later that year in a League game against Partick Thistle. He made two more appearances that season for the first team. The following season Danny played seven more first-team games before being called up for National Service. During the two years he spent in the forces, Danny played for Yeovil Town on loan. On his return to Tynecastle he established himself in the team and will be remembered for his hat-trick in a 4-0 defeat of Hibs in September 1962. As a result of injury problems Danny was freed by Hearts in 1964.

THE SCOTTISH CUP

The Scottish Cup trail began with a trip to East Fife's Bayview Park on 1 February 1958. Two weeks previously Hearts had beaten East Fife 3-0 at the same venue in a League fixture so this particular game appeared to present few problems for the League leaders. The Fifers were anchored near the foot of the League table and their recent form had been dismal in comparison to their visitors. However, the Scottish Cup has been renowned for producing shock results over the years and this one came close. Hearts took the lead through Jimmy Murray after seven minutes but were stunned four minutes later when Neilson equalised. The Edinburgh side were certainly not at their best but still had the bulk of play without converting it into goals. With twenty minutes to go Bobby Blackwood scored what proved to be the winning goal, but East Fife made Hearts fight all the way for the win.

The next round produced a home game against Albion Rovers, and the Coatbridge side were easily seen off by four goals to one. This set up a home game against Hibs in the next round and all of Edinburgh looked forward to what was being described as the capital's biggest game for years. A crowd of 41,666 turned up for the 'Derby' and witnessed a pulsating ninety minutes of football. Johnny Hamilton put Hearts ahead after 20 minutes' play but the lead lasted only two minutes when seventeen-year-old Joe Baker equalised. Baker scored again six minutes later as the Hearts support fell silent. This setback only galvanised Hearts, who stormed the Hibs goal only to find Lawrie Leslie in great form. Jimmy Wardhaugh brought the scores level four minutes into the second half and nearly everyone in the ground now expected Hearts to go on and finish winners. Try as they might, Hearts just couldn't find a way past Leslie in the Hibernian goal and then disaster; Joe Baker completed his hat-trick in the 66th minute and astonishingly scored a fourth with nine minutes remaining. In the final minute Murray scored for Hearts but it was too late and the Cup dream was over.

The disappointment of the Cup exit was soon put aside as Hearts continued their superb League form and on 29 March at home against Raith Rovers another piece of history was made. When Motherwell had clinched the League title in 1931/32, they had scored a record 119 goals in the process. In the game against Raith, Jimmy Murray scored to equal that record and shortly after that Jimmy Wardhaugh headed the ball into the net to create a new record as Hearts ran out 4-1 winners. Life was good down Gorgie way. With only four games remaining in their fixture list it would need a major collapse by Hearts to lose the League. On 5 April Hearts travelled to Rugby Park knowing that victory over Kilmarnock would win them the League. Despite taking the lead through Andy Bowman, an own goal by George Thomson levelled the scores and the game finished 1-1.

The champagne was put on ice for another week. Love Street, Paisley, the home of St Mirren, was the venue for the all-important encounter. The following is a report of the game by Bill Heeps which appeared in the *Edinburgh Evening Dispatch* on Saturday 12 April:

Despite the efforts of Raith Rovers' Andy Leigh and goalkeeper Charlie Drummond, Jimmy Wardhaugh scores the goal to beat Motherwell's record of 119 League goals, which had stood since season 1931/32.

This page: The programme for Hearts' last away game of the season against Aberdeen. The newly crowned Champions of Scotland didn't disappoint their fans in the 12,000 crowd with an emphatic 4-0 win, with goals from Crawford, Wardhaugh, Young and Bowman.

The programme for the last game of the season, against runners-up Rangers on 30 April.

The programme for a trial game for the forthcoming World Cup finals between Hearts and a Scotland XI at Tynecastle.

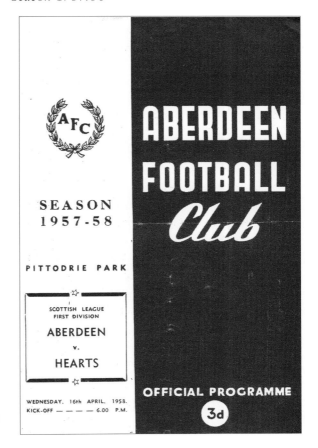

Jimmy Murray comes close as his shot is blocked by Scotland's number 6, Sammy Baird. Hearts won 3-2, the winner coming from Mackay, in front of 30,000 fans in a spectacular game of football.

Gorgie will go gay to-night. The flag is Hearts'. Their two points from St Mirren at Love Street this afternoon gave them the League Championship – the first time they've topped the Division 1 table for sixty-one years. It was a bright, sunny day and the pitch was in excellent order. There was a fast-swelling crowd when the teams came out.

St Mirren: Lornie, Lapsley, McTurk, Neilson, Buchanan, Johnstone, Bryceland, Ryan, Wilson, Gemmell, Miller.
Hearts: Marshall, Kirk, Thomson, Cumming, Milne, Bowman, Blackwood, Murray, Young, Wardhaugh, Crawford.
Referee: H. A. Gallagher, Glasgow.

Hearts had the bulk of the early pressure although they didn't make contact with Lornie. In the seventh minute, they took the lead when lax defending by Lornie and Buchanan allowed Young to score with a tap from close range. Not a spectacular goal but a worthy pay-off for some clock-work football. In the tenth minute, after Cumming had pulled down Gemmell only one yard outside the penalty area, free-kick specialist Davie Lapsley almost shattered the cross-bar with his dead-ball shot. The Maroons almost snatched a second goal when Young found Wardhaugh with

In May 1958 Hearts set off for a tour of Canada and the USA. Pictured at Tynecastle prior to their departure is, back row, left to right: John Cumming, Gordon Marshall, Freddie Glidden, George Thomson, and Billy Higgins.

Middle row, left to right: Alfie Conn, Jimmy Milne, Johnny Hamilton, Bobby Kirk, Bobby Blackwood, Ian Crawford, Willie Lindores, Danny Paton, Jimmy Wardhaugh and Willie Bauld.

Front row, left to right: Andy Bowman, Tommy Walker, Mr. A. Wilson Strachan, Director, Mr. N. G. Kilgour, Chairman, Mr. R. Tait, Director, John Harvey and Alex Young. Missing from the group were Jimmy Murray and Dave Mackay who had been selected for the Scotland squad for the World Cup finals in Sweden.

an inch-perfect pass. However Jimmy's shot was blocked by Buchanan and Lornie completed the clearance. Another brilliant dash by Blackwood, in which he covered sixty yards, was spoiled when Wardhaugh failed to convert his defence-splitting pass. Ten minutes from the interval, Murray, catching a Wardhaugh back-heeler, drove a great shot a foot wide. At the other end Gemmell had a tremendous shot headed away by Milne. Two minutes before the interval, Murray and Young with head and foot respectively just failed to get a second goal.

Half-time: St Mirren 0 – Hearts 1.

Blackwood was having one of his best games and he repeatedly opened up the Paisley defence. Some neat footwork by Wardhaugh in the fifty-third minute bared the defence again but his flashing drive was inches out. In a sharp raid in the fifty-ninth minute Hearts were shocked when a Miller corner was scrambled over the line by Ryan. Within a minute Hearts regained the lead when Wardaugh headed home a Cumming free-kick when Murray had been pulled down on the right. A long-range effort from Murray in the sixty-seventh minute fell into the top net. Then, in another dashing raid Wilson smashed home a brilliant equaliser for St Mirren after Bryceland had laid on a perfect pass. Time, sixty-eight minutes. Hearts were happy again in the seventy-third minute when Young gave them the lead for the third time. A cross from the right was lobbed back in by Crawford and the centre forward touched it past Lornie amid offside appeals which were adamantly refused. Five minutes from the end Bowman was booked for gesturing to the crowd. A Miller 'goal' just after was disallowed for off-side.

Verdict: Not Hearts at their best. But they clinched the flag and their football was always more constructive and more dangerous than the slap-dash raids of St Mirren. It was their team-work once more that counted but there was no denying that Blackwood had a thrilling game. Hearts supporters invaded the pitch after the final whistle to congratulate the new champions.

As expected there was great jubilation in the dressing room after the game as the congratulatory telegrams began to arrive. One of the first was from the Rangers chairman John F. Wilson and the directors, players and staff. It read, 'Heartiest congratulations on winning the Scottish League Championship. Take care of our trophy, we will be after it next year.' The team coach then made its way to the Harp Hotel in Corstorphine for the players and officials to enjoy a well-deserved celebratory meal and drink and to not only reflect on a truly wonderful season but to look forward to the one ahead, when they would take part in the European Cup for the first time.

SEASON 1958/59

The prophetic words of Rangers chairman John F. Wilson – 'Take care of our trophy, we will be after it next year.' – in his telegram to Hearts on winning the League in 1957/58 unfortunately came true. In a dramatic finale to the 1958/59 season, Hearts finished in second place to the Ibrox side and to rub salt into the wounds, Rangers would also claim their scalp in the Scottish Cup. But there was cheer to be found when Tommy Walker's free-flowing side demolished Partick Thistle in the final of the League Cup.

THE LEAGUE CUP

If Hearts were going to win the League Cup it would have to be the hard way, as their sectional teams were Rangers, Raith Rovers and Third Lanark, with the first game being a visit to Ibrox. But the current League holders travelled through to Glasgow that sunny afternoon on 9 August 1958 in a confident mood, and why not? They had beaten Rangers home and away the previous season and Tommy Walker had instilled a strong mentality in the side. Over 60,000 were in the ground for the encounter, such was the drawing power of Hearts. Rangers took the lead through Davie Wilson after 5 minutes and it got worse for Hearts when Johnny Hubbard scored a second on 22 minutes. Any thoughts of a Hearts revival were dispelled when the unfortunate Jimmy Milne put through his own goal just on half-time. Hearts tried hard in the second half but the score remained the same at 3-0. But Hearts simply rolled up their sleeves and the following Wednesday saw them 3-0 victors over Third Lanark, while the same evening Raith Rovers were pulling off a shock result by beating Rangers 3-1 in a bad-tempered match at Stark's Park. Four days later, Hearts took a large support to Kirkcaldy for the meeting with the Rovers. The fans left with grins on their faces at the end of the ninety minutes as they watched their team sweep the Fifers aside in a 3-1 victory. The grins got even wider when they heard that Rangers had been held to a 2-2 draw by Third Lanark at Ibrox. Those results set the scene for yet another showdown between Hearts and Rangers, this one taking place at Tynecastle on 23 August. This game had it all as 42,000 fans watched a drama-packed match unfold. A game which threw up injuries to both sets of players, with the Rangers goalkeeper Norrie Martin being taken off with a

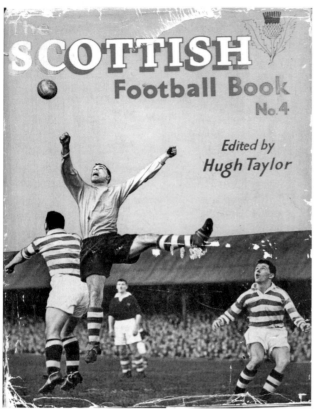

This page: *The Scottish Football Book 1958/59.*

Programme for the Hearts *v.* Third Lanark League Cup game on 13 August.

Programme for the Rangers *v.* Hearts League Cup game on 9 August.

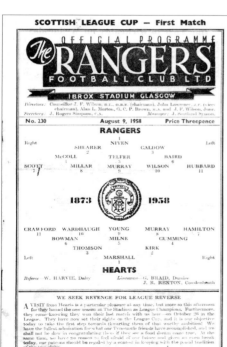

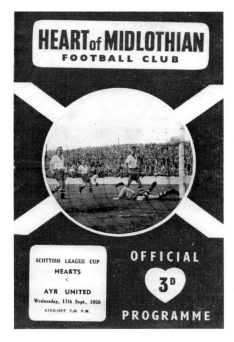

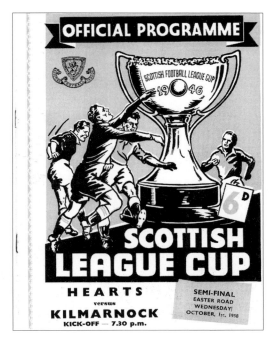

Above left: Programme for the second leg quarter-final League Cup tie against Ayr United.

Above right: Programme for the semi-final game against Kilmarnock at Easter Road on 1 October.

broken collar bone, fierce tackling by each side as no quarter was given, disturbances on the terracing resulting in numerous arrests being made by 'Edinburgh's Finest', missiles being thrown onto the pitch and an injury-time winner by Jimmy Milne to send the Hearts support into raptures. In the remaining two fixtures Third Lanark and Raith Rovers were beaten 5-4 and 3-1 respectively as the Tynecastle men secured their place in the quarter-finals. In the two-legged tie Ayr United were beaten home and away 5-1 and 3-1 as Hearts marched into the semi-finals to face Kilmarnock at Easter Road. A crowd of just over 41,000 saw Hearts see off the Ayrshire men with goals from Thomson, Crawford and Bauld.

THE LEAGUE CUP FINAL 1958/59

Partick Thistle were Hearts' opponents in the final. The 'Jags' were a mercurial side who could scale great heights in one game, sending their support into raptures, only to drive the same fans to despair in the next fixture with a performance so inept that it would beggar belief. Their fans sometimes endured endless encounters which would have sent other supporters either to sleep or the madhouse. They had various nicknames bestowed upon them such as the 'Harry Wraggs' or the tongue-in-cheek 'Maryhill Magyars' but nobody in football had a harsh word to say about Thistle. This was a team who had to live in a city also occupied by Celtic and Rangers and

Programme for the 1958/59 League Cup
final.

were viewed as the alternative club in Glasgow, with a support that did not have great
expectations, just the love of football. In the other semi-final Partick had defeated
the more fancied Celtic, who had been the previous year's winners, so the question
was, because of their inconsistency, which Thistle team would turn up at Hampden
for the final? The omens leading up to the game weren't good for Thistle as the
previous week Hearts had defeated them 2-0 in a League game in Edinburgh and
added to that, they would be without their top goalscorer Andy Kerr through injury.
By contrast Hearts had no problems and went into the game as League leaders.

The team line-ups were:

Hearts: Marshall, Kirk, Thomson, Mackay, Glidden, Cumming, Hamilton, Murray,
Bauld, Wardhaugh, Crawford.
Partick Thistle: Ledgerwood, Hogan, Donlevy, Mathers, Davidson, Wright,
Mackenzie, Thomson, Smith, McParland, Ewing.
Referee: R. H. Davidson, Airdrie.

In Edinburgh's *Evening Dispatch*, reporter Jimmy Cowe gave this report:

With only 15 minutes to go before the kick-off, no more than 30,000 fans were on
the terracing. Hearts arrived 45 minutes before the kick-off, 10 seconds behind a
smiling, cheery bunch of Partick players who didn't seem to mind being quoted as
3-1 outsiders by the Glasgow bookies. Happiest man as the teams took the field?
Undoubtedly Davie Mathers, captain of Partick, who was hoping to celebrate his
27th birthday with a win. Hearts won the toss, the bands of the Cameronians

and Kosbies played 'The Queen' and Smith set the ball rolling. Hearts fans were not long in getting their lungs into action and a Supporters' Club banner waved into action on the East terracing. Banners in Glasgow? Tut, Tut! Three corners in three minutes and a goal in the fourth. How that banner waved as Bauld slipped home Murray's cross and how the Partick players wanted the linesman to wave his 'banner' for offside. Murray was the menace to Partick's peace of mind. His positioning was perfect and how he made a great job of Bobby Kirk's slip through in the 9th minute. Ledgerwood's dash out was merely a token gesture as No. 2 rolled into the net. Frankly Partick weren't in the hunt in the opening 15 minutes. Shades of M.C.C. down under as it looked like being a cricket score. Mackay, Glidden and Cumming, half-back veterans of the 1954 League Cup success had gained a quick stranglehold. The crowd, now of reasonable dimensions, applauded the sock-em-hard Hearts. A tendency to off-side was Hearts' one fault – lucky for this easy-split Partick defence. With 27 minutes gone Hearts went further ahead. Crawford's corner kick, the neat header of Murray and Bauld's flick home from two yards suggested that the next 63 minutes would be a mere formality. But what is this? Thirty two minutes gone and Partick daring to have a shot at goal. McParland did the trick but Marshall trumped it with a great save. Just to show them they had no right to do that Hearts scored No.4. Yes, Murray it was and I had to sympathise with Partick. Jimmy looked off-side when Hamilton passed. The linesman flagged and Partick hesitated. No whistle came until Murray's left foot shot was in the net and Mr Davidson wouldn't change his mind.

Half-time: Hearts 4 – Partick Thistle 0.

A little laddie decked out in a maroon tammy and tracksuit expressed the thoughts of the crowd when he toddled onto the field to present Gordon Marshall with a replica of the Cup. Then, sensation in the fifty-sixth minute – a goal for Partick and it really wakened them up. They fought like furies for the first time in the game and Hearts were almost panicking in defence. But the magic of Murray soon disposed of any Firhill hopes of recovery. He backheeled beautifully for Hamilton's net bulging contribution in the sixty-ninth minute. Eight minutes from time Murray was downed in the box. Did I detect a note of leniency when Mr Davidson waved play on? Strange thing about this 'no contest' Final was that Partick had actually 13 corners to Hearts 10. But Hearts were ahead in the most important point of all.

Attendance: 59,960.

Verdict: A fantastic final. Partick were so pitifully poor, there probably has never been a more one-sided final in the history of the competition. The makeshift Firhill side were completely outclassed by a Tynecastle team which ticked over like a well-oiled machine. But the foundation of Hearts' third cup success in four years was laid in the strength of the half-back line and the complete dominance of Mackay and Cumming over the Firhill inside forwards. Partick did show a bit more fight in the second half with Ewing trying hard all the time to link up the attack but there was really no chance of them making a comeback against these throbbing Hearts. The only Thistle men to escape criticism in this debacle were Mathers, Ledgerwood, Hogan, Smith and Ewing.

THE EUROPEAN CUP

Hearts' first venture into the European Cup as Champions of Scotland began with an away tie in Belgium against Standard Liège on 3 September 1958. Despite taking an early lead through Ian Crawford they found themselves 2-1 down at the interval. Hearts continued to play attacking football in the second half, which was to prove costly as the Belgians picked them off, scoring a further three goals in the last eighteen minutes, making the return leg in Edinburgh an uphill task. But a crowd of 39,000 were inside the ground the following week and saw their side putting up a spirited performance, with Bauld scoring twice in a 2-1 win, restoring a bit of pride. Amazingly, the following evening Hearts had to travel to Somerset Park to play the first leg of the League Cup quarter-finals against Ayr United.

THE LEAGUE CHAMPIONSHIP

Dunfermline Athletic were the visitors to Tynecastle for a three o'clock kick-off on 20 August for the first League game of the season. By quarter-to-five that afternoon they were probably regretting making the trip from Fife as Hearts walloped them 6-2. Hearts' rich vein of League form continued until 1 November, when a very fine Motherwell side gave them their first League defeat of the season. Willie Hunter and Pat Quinn inflicted the damage for the 'Steelmen' in a 2-0 victory, with both goals coming in the last two minutes of the game. This win put Motherwell into second place in the League, just one point behind Hearts.

The players responded well to the defeat by Motherwell and on 13 December they travelled through to Govan to play Rangers as League leaders, two points ahead of the Ibrox men. Rangers themselves had struck form and lay in second place behind Hearts. Another large attendance was expected for the fixture between the best two sides in Scotland at that time. Hearts were hit by injuries before the game and Tommy Walker was forced to give George Robertson his first competitive debut in a maroon jersey in the centre half position. Robertson had only signed for Hearts in June of that year from Tranent Juniors and was literally thrown in at the deep-end for this vital fixture. From the start Hearts took the game to Rangers and in the first minute Alex Young hit the post but two minutes later Ralph Brand, himself an Edinburgh lad, put the 'Light Blues' ahead. Twenty minutes later the Hearts support in the 66,000 crowd couldn't believe what was happening as centre forward Max Murray of Rangers had by this time completed his hat-trick as Hearts trailed 4-0. Murray was certainly taking advantage of the unfortunate Robertson's inexperience in defence. The roof had well and truly caved in on Hearts when Brand scored again in the 34th minute. The Tynecastle men tried all they could in the second half but the score remained the same. The effect of this defeat at the hands of Rangers was there for all to see as Hearts won only one League game in the next five, which included a 3-1 home defeat by Hibs on New Year's day and a 4-1 humiliation to low-placed Stirling Albion a few weeks later.

The Standard Liège defenders watch this shot go past in the second-leg tie at Tynecastle.

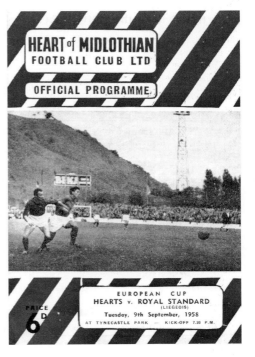

The away and home programme publications for the European Cup games against Royal Standard Liège of Belgium.

Top: Third Lanark's goalkeeper George Ramage holds the ball from the onrushing Jimmy Murray, watched by Third's Willie Cunningham in the League game played on 27 September. Some of Hearts' play was stunning in the 8-3 mauling, with Willie Bauld scoring five of the goals.

Above: Murray has a great view of one of the eight goals. John Lewis is the Third Lanark number 5.

Determination is written on Bauld's face as he crashes home one of his five goals in the rout.

THE SCOTTISH CUP

In the week following the defeat to Stirling Albion, Queen of the South were beaten 3-1 in the first round of the Scottish Cup at Palmerston. Two weeks later Hearts' progress was halted in the competition when Rangers knocked them out with a 3-2 win at Ibrox.

But the team recovered some League form after those setbacks and began to put results together again, with morale returning to the dressing room. Then came the bombshell. On 8 March, the fans' favourite, Dave Mackay, was transferred to Tottenham Hotspur for a sum reported to be £32,000. The support were stunned at Mackay's departure and were of the view that his move south would have an adverse effect on Hearts retaining the League Championship. The Hearts followers still harboured thoughts of overtaking Rangers in the League race but with the going of Mackay they were now of the opinion that any slim hope of catching them had gone. When Mackay left for London, Hearts trailed Rangers by six points but had played one game less.

Gordon Marshall smothers a shot from Max Murray of Rangers, watched by Jimmy Milne, Bobby Kirk and Ralph Brand in the Scottish Cup on 14 February, 1959 in front of 55,000 fans.

Bobby Kirk puts through his own goal in the seventeenth minute to give Rangers a 2-1 lead as Rangers' Max Murray jumps with joy.

Alex Young challenges Rangers' George Niven in quagmire conditions that Rangers adapted to much better than their visitors.

Dave Mackay with John Harvey. In 1952 Dave arrived at Tynecastle from junior side Newtongrange Star and made his debut on 7 November of the following year in a League match against Clyde. He quickly became a fans' favourite with his spirit, will-to-win attitude and robust style of play. Mackay never knew the meaning of the word defeat as he contested every ball. He was imperious as he strode across the football field, chest puffed out, encouraging his team-mates, distributing passes with unerring accuracy and those qualities, coupled with his tenacity in the tackle, made him a formidable opponent. The news of his transfer to Tottenham Hotspur in March 1959 stunned the fans, coming a month after he had been awarded the 1958 Footballer of the Year trophy at a packed Usher Hall. The Spurs manager Bill Nicholson had long admired Dave's attributes and saw him as a vital component in his side, playing alongside Danny Blanchflower at White Hart Lane. Nicholson's judgement was proved correct as Spurs won the Football League Championship and the FA Cup in season 1960/61, ably assisted by the irrepressible Mackay. During his time at Spurs Mackay suffered leg breaks on two occasions but still came back fighting. Brian Clough took Mackay to Derby County in 1968 while they were in the Second Division and what a shrewd signing it turned out to be as 'The Rams' won promotion at the end of season 1968/69. Dave was awarded the Football Writers' Player of the Year for 1969 at the age of thirty-four years, an honour richly deserved.

Opposite above: Mackay was capped for his country on twenty-two occasions and is seen here in a Scotland team to face Northern Ireland at Windsor Park, Belfast in October 1959, which the Scots won 4-0.

Back, left to right: Eric Caldow, Bobby Evans, Bill Brown, Dave Mackay, Bert McCann, John Hewie. Front, left to right: Graham Leggat, John White, Ian St John, Denis Law and George Mulhall.

Opposite below: One of Mackay's worst footballing experiences while playing for Scotland was the 9-3 drubbing by England on 15 April 1961 at Wembley. The squad are pictured here at Euston Railway Station, London on the morning of the game, having travelled down on the overnight train. Left to right: Denis Law, Billy McNeill, Davie Wilson, Bobby Shearer, Frank Haffey, Duncan McKay, Johnny McLeod, Pat Quinn, Bert McCann, Eric Caldow, Dave Mackay and Ian St John. The story goes that on their arrival at Wembley the team were walking across the playing surface, which was like the proverbial bowling green, when Dave said, 'Lads if we canny play on a pitch like this the day, then we'll never play.'

Above: Cathkin Park, Glasgow, 25 February 1959, and Hearts are on the defensive. John Lough clears his lines from Third Lanark's Bobby Craig. Hearts won 4-0 with goals from George Thomson (3) and Johnny Hamilton.

As it transpired, Mackay's leaving didn't overly affect the team at that time and they continued to snap at the heels of Rangers, who by this time were dropping vital points. With three games left to play in the campaign, Hearts were six points behind their rivals, with Rangers set to visit Tynecastle on 11 April. To all intents and purposes it was the Championship decider, with a draw enabling Rangers to be crowned Champions on Hearts territory. But the 'Maroons' were having none of that and set about Rangers from the first whistle in front of a crowd of 30,000. On the same day Scotland were facing England at Wembley in the Home Internationals and thousands of Scots were in London for the game. In those days it was something of a pilgrimage to travel across the border to face the 'Auld Enemy' and wasn't to be missed at any cost, hence the lower than normal attendance at Tynecastle. In an ill-tempered game John Cumming gave his side the lead in the thirty-second minute when he took a pass from George Thomson to steer the ball wide of George Niven in the Rangers goal. The referee, Mr G. Bowman, was a busy man as both sides endeavoured to kick lumps out of each other, sometimes with the ball elsewhere. With fifteen minutes remaining, Bobby Rankin, a recent signing from Queen of the South, put the game to bed with a second goal. Tynecastle went wild. Hearts then defeated Aberdeen 4-2 in midweek.

Now only two points separated them with, incredibly, both teams having the same goal average. The last game took Hearts to the east end of Glasgow to face Celtic while Rangers entertained Aberdeen at Ibrox Stadium. Nowadays, the scenario of two games taking place in Glasgow at the same time to decide the destiny of the League Championship would not be permitted by the authorities. Rangers had only to draw to secure the League and by a strange twist of fate Aberdeen had to win to avoid relegation. Hearts began well and it was no surprise when Bobby Rankin put them ahead after 25 minutes. Meanwhile, over on the south side of the city Rangers led by a similar score courtesy of a Ralph Brand goal. Hearts were well in control of their game and were looking to increase their lead but the score remained the same at the interval. But at Ibrox, the unthinkable had happened. Aberdeen had equalised through Norrie Davidson just before half-time. Could the 'Dons' do the nigh impossible and beat Rangers, leaving Hearts as Champions if their score with Celtic remained the same? Five minutes into the second half Norrie Davidson gave his side the lead over Rangers and as it stood Hearts would retain the League. Things were looking good. Then disaster struck. Bertie Auld equalised for Celtic in the 53rd minute and worse was to follow when Eric Smith put the 'Hoops' ahead after 67 minutes. Hearts began to fall apart and were all over the place as Celtic now dictated the run of play. It was probably at that point that nearly everyone connected to Hearts realised just how much the team missed the tenacity and spirit of the barrel-chested Dave Mackay as the 'Gorgie' men slumped to defeat and threw away a League Championship on the final day of the season. Unfortunately, this would not be the last time that this would happen to Hearts, but that's another story for another day in the history of the club. Would Hearts have retained the League title if Mackay had stayed at Tynecastle? That's a question which will forever remain unanswered.

SEASON 1959/60

When older fans of Hearts talk about football, 1959/60 is invariably mentioned. At the end of the season the League Championship flag would return to Gorgie as Tommy Walker's troops played some quite amazing football throughout. Kilmarnock, not Rangers, would emerge as the main challengers to their title hopes and the Ayrshire men would give Hearts a run for their money in the weeks leading up to the season's finale. The League Cup would be retained to adorn the trophy cabinet in the Tynecastle boardroom as Hearts enjoyed their most successful season in the club's history. In the Scottish Cup Kilmarnock, managed by the ex-Ranger Willie Waddell, would put paid to any thoughts of a 'Treble' by putting them out of the competition and only after a replay. But a surprise awaited the 'Maroon Faithful' before a ball had been kicked in earnest when news broke that Gordon Smith, who had been given a free transfer by Hibernian, had signed for Hearts. More than a few eyebrows were raised at the thirty-four-year-old's signing but Tommy Walker viewed his arrival as a 'good piece of work'. Despite his previous curriculum vitae, Gordon was welcomed on-board.

THE LEAGUE CUP

Hearts opened their League Cup sectional game on 8 August with a devastating display of football as Kilmarnock were simply swept aside in a 4-0 defeat at Rugby Park. The midweek home game against Aberdeen was a bit of a disappointment as the 'Dons' returned north with a valuable point from a 2-2 draw, but the smiles were soon back on the faces of the fans when two goals by Ian Crawford saw off Stirling Albion at Annfield. The following week Gordon Smith made his competitive debut in a 2-0 win over Kilmarnock at Tynecastle. Following that victory, Hearts made the long trip north to the 'Granite City' to face a vastly improving Aberdeen side. This was a crucial game for both teams as they shared top spot in the section, and the winners of this game would almost certainly qualify for the quarter-final stages of the tournament. The match programme notes alluded to this and a good attendance was anticipated inside Pittodrie. A crowd of 31,000 saw Hearts put on another fine display in a 4-1 win, with Gordon Smith scoring his first ever goal for his new side. The final game of the section finished with a 2-2 draw against Stirling Albion, with Jimmy Murray netting twice.

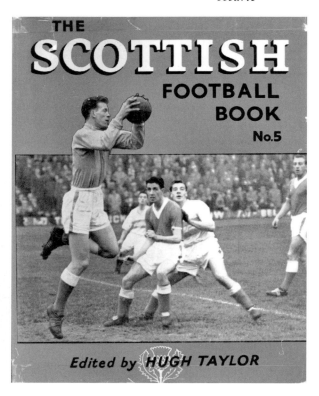

Left: The Scottish Football Book 1959/60.

Below: Jimmy Brown brings off a save in the League Cup game at Rugby Park on 8 August. Bobby Kennedy of Kilmarnock and Jimmy Wardhaugh are also photographed.

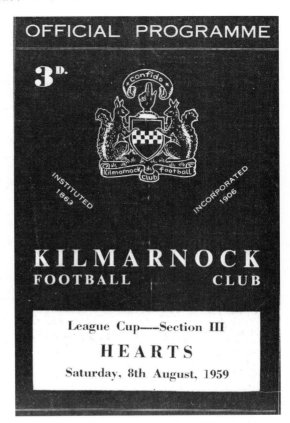

Right: Programme for the opening
League Cup game at Rugby Park,
8 August 1959.

Below: Programmes for Hearts v.
Kilmarnock & Aberdeen v. Hearts on 22
and 28 August.

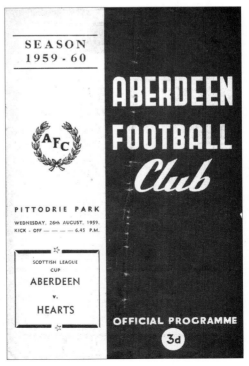

OFFICIAL PROGRAMME

(First published. August, 1948)

Motherwell F.C.

SEASON 1959-60

No. 5   *Price Threepence*

SCOTTISH LEAGUE CUP—QUARTER FINAL (1st Leg)

MOTHERWELL
versus
HEARTS

FIR PARK, MOTHERWELL

WEDNESDAY, SEPTEMBER 9, 1959   Kick-off 7.15 p.m.

HEART of MIDLOTHIAN

FOOTBALL CLUB

Official Programme

Scottish League Cup

HEARTS v MOTHERWELL   3D

WEDNESDAY, 16th SEPTEMBER, 1959
KICK-OFF 7.30 P.M.

Above, left and right: The programmes for the quarter-final League Cup games against Motherwell.

The quarter-final draw saw Hearts travel to Lanarkshire for the first leg to face Motherwell. The 'Steelmen' had finished with full points in their section, which contained Dundee, Hibs and Rangers. Both the victories over Rangers were no flukes and under manager Bobby Ancell they were a marvellous and entertaining side to watch, always intent on playing the ball on the ground. The forward line of Willie Hunter, Sammy Reid, Ian St John, Pat Quinn and Andy Weir was a joy to be seen when in full flight. Due to the massive interest in the game a huge crowd turned up at Fir Park, causing the turnstiles to be closed before kick-off time, resulting in many fans being locked out of the ground. On a beautiful sunny autumn evening, the Motherwell forward line immediately clicked into gear as they took the game to their opponents. In the opening stages Motherwell scorned some good chances to take the lead. But Hearts had their chances as well and only a goal-line clearance from Bert McCann prevented them going ahead. Motherwell were then punished for their earlier misses when Blackwood scored for the visitors. A through pass from Gordon Smith put Jimmy Wardhaugh in behind the Motherwell defence; Jimmy's shot rebounded from the post but only to Bobby Blackwood, who easily netted.

Programme for the League Cup
semi-final played on 9 October at
Easter Road.

Just before the interval St John equalised for the 'Well and it was now 'game on'. Roared on by the big crowd, both teams put on a show worthy of the occasion from undoubtedly the finest two footballing sides in Scotland at that time. Play raged from end to end without anyone gaining supremacy and honours were even at the end. The players left the field to rapturous applause from both sets of fans, who knew they had witnessed a football feast. The following morning the footballing press used up all the superlatives to describe the match. The eagerly awaited return leg took place the following week on 16 September in front of another huge crowd, thought to be in the region of 44,000. In an electric-charged atmosphere under the powerful Tynecastle floodlights, Alex Young gave his team the lead in the very first minute. The stadium was a wall of sound as Hearts tried to add to their lead but that man St John, who would join Liverpool the following season, popped up again to equalise for the 'Fir Parkers'. Any thoughts of Motherwell pulling off a famous victory quickly vanished as Bobby Blackwood scored twice before the interval to give Hearts a 3-1 lead. Motherwell had a mountain to climb going into the second half which became insurmountable when Alex Young and Johnny Hamilton scored again for Hearts. To their credit, Motherwell didn't give up and St John scored a second but in the final minute Jimmy Murray put another one away to make it 6-2 on the night and 7-3 on aggregate. In the semi-final Cowdenbeath were beaten 9-3 at Easter Road on 9 October as the Tynecastle machine rolled on to the final, where they would meet Third Lanark.

THE LEAGUE CUP FINAL 1959/60

Hearts: Marshall, Kirk, Thomson, Bowman, Cumming, Higgins, Smith, Crawford, Young, Blackwood, Hamilton.
Third Lanark: Robertson, Lewis, Brown, Reilly, McCallum, Cunningham, McInnes, Craig, D. Hilley, Gray, I. Hilley.
Referee: T. Wharton, Glasgow.

For the final it was a dull afternoon and Hampden Park looked stark, stern and grey as the fans made their way into the stadium. The ground was infamous for what was known as the Hampden Swirl. It was a spiteful wind which, at its worst, rushed down the park to the east end of the ground, making ball control difficult. It could suddenly come to life in the goalmouth area without warning, leaving many a goalkeeper looking foolish when dealing with cross balls. With only two and a half minutes of the game gone, it did just that. Out on the right wing Third Lanark's Joe McInnes had the ball. Almost contemptuously, he tricked George Thomson and then drifted a speculative lob into the goalmouth area. The wind seemed to carry the ball towards Gordon Marshall, who rose up took take the ball with ease. Did he misjudge his leap? Did the notorious Hampden Swirl, in full blast that day, come in to take the ball away from him? Did he lose sight of the ball? Whatever the reason, Gordon merely touched the ball into the air. It came down behind him and as he made a frantic effort to recover, Third's Matt Gray reacted quickly to the situation to put the ball over the line. The Hearts fans in the crowd of almost 58,000 were stunned as their favourites went behind. The response to this setback was instant as Walker's men began to bombard the Thirds' goal, where 'keeper Jocky Robertson was performing heroics as he kept them at bay. Robertson, the smallest goalkeeper in Scotland, was immense as Hearts threatened to overrun his defence. Full-length saves, one-handed saves, tipping shots round the post or over the bar, you name it – Jocky did it. Meanwhile, with the wind behind them, Third Lanark could only rely on counter attacks which were dealt with effectively by the Hearts defenders. They did get a fright when a header from Gray went narrowly past, but by and large Third weren't posing a threat. When Tom Wharton's whistle brought the first half to a close Jocky Robertson received a cheer all to himself as he made his way to the dressing-room. Edinburgh born, he was a life-long Hearts fan and here he was breaking their fans' hearts. The pattern of play in the second half mirrored the first – Hearts *v.* Robertson. Inside the first few minutes the Gorgie side mounted one of the most sustained barrages Hampden Park has ever witnessed as they attacked with bewildering speed but the Hi Hi stood firm. On 57 minutes Hearts got their reward when Johnny Hamilton struck a shot from 22 yards which took a slight deflection of Third Lanark's McCallum before ending up in the net. The relief of the Hearts players was obvious as they celebrated the goal. Two minutes later it was all over as Alex Young outwitted the Third Lanark defence and shot past Robertson from eight yards. A mixture of missed chances by Hearts and resolute defending by Third Lanark saw an end to the scoring. The

Above left: Gordon Marshall loses the flight of the ball as Matt Gray waits to score in the opening minutes of the game.

Above right: The 1959/60 League Cup final programme showing an aerial view of Hampden Park.

Glasgow side had put up a tremendous fight but no one could deny Hearts their richly deserved victory.

After the League Cup success the congratulations and good wishes that poured in from all over the country were many and varied. Among the first congratulations were telegrams from two former Hearts captains, Freddie Glidden and Bobby Parker, and one from the Hibs manager, Hugh Shaw. Longstone Hearts Supporters Club indulged in a bit of forecasting when they sent their good wishes as they anticipated the Treble. The message read: 'Our congratulations on winning the Cup. We will follow on with the League Flag and the Scottish Cup.'

Sadly, less than eight years after the League Cup final Third Lanark ceased to exist, just five years away from the club's centenary. The downfall was brought about by a variety of reasons, mismanagement and other dark deeds behind the scenes. To this day Third Lanark are remembered with great affection when older fans recall some of the games they saw on their travels to Cathkin Park. On 28 April 1967, Third Lanark played their last ever game in Scottish football when they were defeated 5-1 by Dumbarton. It is quite ironic that their goal was scored by Drew Busby who, in

Left: This is thought to be the last photograph of Third Lanark, which was taken at Douglas Park, Hamilton on 21 August 1965. The goalkeeper, Evan Williams, would later play for Celtic and appear in the European Cup final for them in 1970 against Feyenoord.

Below: The official party make their way through the streets of 'Auld Reekie'.

later years, would join up at Tynecastle, where he would become a legend in the eyes of the Hearts fans. Liquidators were called in to investigate the running of the club but in June of that year the gates of Cathkin Park were closed and locked and a once great and proud club disappeared from the beautiful game.

THE LEAGUE CHAMPIONSHIP

Dens Park, Dundee was the first port of call when the 1959/60 League campaign began on 19 August. Two goals from Hamilton and another from Cumming were enough to see off Dundee in a 3-1 win. Next up were Hibernian, who had made a poor start to the season, and that run was expected to continue given both sides' current form. But the unexpected usually happens in derby games and this one was no exception as Hibs returned to Leith with a point after Joe Baker had scored both their goals in a 2-2 draw. Hearts had chances to see off their rivals but ran out of luck in front of goal and had a double from Jimmy Murray to thank for securing the draw.

They got a fright at Celtic Park the following week. With only 21 minutes on the clock Hamilton, Murray and Young had put Hearts into a three-goal lead and were simply cruising going in at the interval. However, they contrived to throw away this

An action shot from the League game on 3 October at Tynecastle against newly promoted Ayr United. Hearts won 5-3 with goals from Young (2) Murray, Smith and Blackwood.

Above: In the same game Gordon Smith reacts angrily to a tackle by an Ayr United defender.

Left: On 10 October Hearts defeated Airdrie 5-2 at Broomfield. Airdrie's Jock Wallace is pictured making a save watched by Doug Baillie, the Airdrie centre half, and Johnny Hamilton. 'Wee Hammy', as he was affectionately known by the support, was one of the most popular players ever to play for Hearts. Signed in April 1955, he made his competitive debut later that year in a League game against Airdrie. He was a live-wire of a player and his amazing bursts of speed left defenders in his wake as he went on his runs down the wing. Although only 5'6", he could look after himself on the pitch and he feared no one. Johnny won every honour with Hearts and the fans were sad to see him go in April 1967 when he left for Watford.

advantage and with twenty minutes remaining Celtic had levelled the score with goals from Auld, Divers and Conway. Roared on by their support, the 'Hoops' were now looking for the winner. With three minutes remaining Bobby Blackwood silenced them when he scored Hearts' fourth goal. This win demonstrated the resilience that this Hearts side possessed and sent a clear warning to the other teams in the League of their intentions to be crowned champions come the end of the season.

The week following the League Cup triumph the Hearts support returned to Glasgow with high hopes for the vital clash with Rangers at Ibrox. Hearts were undefeated in the nine League games played and sat top, two points clear of Rangers who were in second place. Rangers had made an indifferent start to the League, suffering home defeats by newly promoted Ayr United and Scottish Cup holders St Mirren. But they were still a force to be reckoned with and Hearts knew they would have to be at their best to get anything out of the game. Just before kick-off a loudspeaker message was read out warning young fans not to come onto the field of play to get autographs. It was a dull, gloomy day with drizzling rain falling as the teams emerged from the dressing rooms, with Hearts remaining unchanged from the previous week. Despite the weather 72,000 fans turned up to watch what they hoped would be a spectacle, and they weren't disappointed.

Rangers: Niven, Shearer, Caldow, Davis, Paterson, Stevenson, Scott, McMillan, Millar, Brand, Matthew.
Hearts: Marshall, Kirk, Thomson, Bowman, Cumming, Higgins, Smith, Crawford, Young, Blackwood, Hamilton.
Referee: Mr J. Rodger, Stonehouse.

Rangers made a whirlwind start and after only thirty seconds Bobby Kirk was forced to concede a corner. From the resultant kick a nervous-looking Gordon Marshall punched the ball straight out to Rangers' Brand, whose shot was cleared off the line by Kirk. A few minutes later Hearts survived another moment of panic when sloppy defending allowed Brand to slip in behind them, but he just failed to reach the ball with the goal at his mercy. Ibrox Stadium was a cauldron of noise as the Rangers support urged their team on. Then, right out of the blue, Hearts took the lead in the eighth minute. They won a corner on the right and when the ball came straight to Crawford, who was unmarked, he made a sorry hash of a great chance. But then Davis, in attempting to clear, smashed the ball against his team mate Shearer and the ball went away from Niven and into the net. Play then went from end to end, with Brand heading past an empty goal and then Hamilton doing likewise for Hearts when it seemed easier to score. The Ibrox men then missed a series of golden opportunities and should have equalised but the Hearts goal remained intact. Just on half-time George Niven pulled off a fantastic save from a Johnny Hamilton shot, touching the ball onto the bar. Rangers dominated the second half and at times Hearts were hemmed inside their own eighteen-yard box, but with a few minutes remaining Bobby Blackwood put the game beyond doubt with a second goal to put the Edinburgh side four points clear at the top of the League. Hearts' great run of form continued through November before they suffered back-to-back defeats to St Mirren and Motherwell during December.

On New Year's Day 1960 Hearts first-footed Hibernian at Easter Road and showed no 'festive spirit' to their neighbours with an emphatic 5-1 victory over their great rivals. An Alex Young hat-trick, an own goal by Plenderleith, and, to rub salt into the already gaping Hibs wounds, a goal by former favourite son Gordon Smith rounded off a perfect day for the Hearts support. The following day Celtic came calling in Gorgie and they also received no 'compliments of the season' from Hearts as they were sent back to the east end of Glasgow empty-handed after a 3-1 defeat.

Left: Ian Crawford shoots for goal in the 2-0 triumph over Rangers.

Below: Harold Davis of Rangers can only look on in horror as his attempted clearance hits Bobby Shearer and spins away from George Niven to put Hearts one up.

Above: During the League game against Rangers on 9 March 1960, Ian Crawford runs in on Rangers' George Niven.

Right: The League Championship souvenir pennant for 1959/60.

LEAGUE CHAMPIONS HEARTS 1959-1960

CUMMING (CAPT.)
BROWN · KIRK
YOUNG · BAULD
BOWMAN · MILNE
CRAWFORD · SMITH
McFADZEAN
THOMSON
MARSHALL
HAMILTON
BLACKWOOD
MURRAY
HIGGINS

Gordon Marshall hits the ground after tipping a shot over the bar in the game with Kilmarnock at Rugby Park on 19 March 1960.

Going into January, Kilmarnock struck a rich vein of form and had hauled themselves up the League and were now, along with Rangers, challenging Hearts. During that month Hearts had drawn three of the six games played, allowing Kilmarnock to close the gap on them. On 6 February the team got back on track with a hard-earned 3-2 win over Airdrieonians at Tynecastle, but because of bad weather and Scottish Cup commitments, wouldn't play another League game for three weeks.

THE SCOTTISH CUP

In the Scottish Cup Hearts received a bye into the second round and were drawn at home against Kilmarnock. The game was scheduled for 13 February but was postponed due to Tynecastle being snowbound. There were a further two postponements before the game got underway on the evening of Monday 22nd. Despite the pitch having a light covering of snow, the teams served up thrilling cup fare and gave the 33,889 crowd an outstanding evening's entertainment. Hearts found themselves a goal down to Kilmarnock at the interval, with Billy Muir scoring for the Ayrshire side, but Alex Young equalised in the second half to keep the Cup hopes alive. It was a game that Hearts should have won given the amount of pressure they had applied, but it was not to be. The replay took place two days later in front of a crowd of 24,359. The adjective 'epic' was applied to the replay by nearly every newspaper in the country. It was indeed a pity that one of the teams had to lose and unfortunately it had to be Hearts. Ian Crawford struck the bar with a vicious shot in the opening stages but Billy Muir once again gave his side the lead, this time through a penalty. A goal by Jimmy Murray drew Hearts level in the second half and twice the woodwork came to 'Killie's rescue as they sought the winner. With four minutes to go, tragedy struck when Rab Stewart scored for Kilmarnock, bringing the curtain down on an enthralling game and ending the Longstone Hearts Supporters Club's dream of a 'Treble'. Kilmarnock would progress to the final of the Scottish Cup on 23 April, only to go down 2-0 to Rangers.

Hearts didn't hang about feeling sorry for themselves and Third Lanark suffered the backlash in a 4-1 defeat at Cathkin Park following on from the Cup exit. 5 March bought another crucial game to Tynecastle in the shape of the visit of Rangers. Scot Symon's side had dropped to third place in the League behind Kilmarnock after drawing with Aberdeen at Ibrox on 1 March. Defeat by Hearts would all but end any chance of them retaining the League title. In front of another big crowd Rangers had the better of the earlier play and could have taken the lead, but Hearts began to assert themselves through Cumming and Higgins. It was all square at the interval and in the second half tempers started to flare on and off the pitch, with Edinburgh City Police kept busy with sporadic outbursts of trouble on the terracing. With 9 minutes to go, Hearts broke the deadlock with a quite magnificent strike by John Cumming. The Hearts fans were still celebrating when Alex Young scored a second. From the kick-off Ian McMillan attempted a wide pass out to Alex Scott on the wing but Johnny Hamilton intercepted it and played Alex Young in. Alex simply glided in on goal, drew Niven from his goal line and then calmly steered the ball into the net. The huge following of Rangers fans made their way towards the exits, knowing that their team's chances were dead and buried. In stark contrast, the Hearts fans were celebrating wildly as a state of bedlam ensued within the ground. Surely now the League was won. With seven games remaining they were five points clear of nearest challengers Kilmarnock. Wins over Arbroath and Partick Thistle brought the Championship nearer. But Kilmarnock were still hanging in there and the visit by Hearts to Rugby Park on 19 March was now vital to both sides. The Hearts support travelled down the A71 Edinburgh–Kilmarnock road knowing that victory would put paid to 'Killie's title hopes. Alas, Kilmarnock hadn't read that particular script. The importance of the fixture was reflected in the attendance of 26,584, which was Kilmarnock's biggest crowd of the season. Right from the start the game was ablaze and both sides made early chances. A tremendous shot by Ian Crawford beat Jimmy Brown in goal and almost shattered the crossbar. It was the 'Maroons' who were in control and were by now playing devastating football. In the 20th minute an Alex Young effort was heading for the net when Kilmarnock defender Matt Watson made a diving save and beat the ball down with both hands. Watson was allowed to remain on the field as back then this offence didn't warrant a booking, never mind a red card as would happen today. George Thomson stepped up to take the resultant penalty and just before the kick was taken Jimmy Brown appeared to move to his left. Thomson sent the ball to the opposite side of goal but it went wide of the post to a great roar of relief from the Kilmarnock fans and groans of despair from the Hearts contingent. In the 16th minute of the second half Hearts scored what looked like a flag-winning goal. A lob up-field from George Thomson completely deceived Kilmarnock's Willie Toner. The ball landed at Ian Crawford's feet, who simply picked his spot. The Championship look lasted all of two minutes, when Jackie McInally equalised with a header. With a few minutes till the final whistle, and nearly everyone inside the ground settling for a draw, George Thomson's nightmare continued when he handled the ball in the penalty area. Billy Muir made no mistake with the spot-kick to give Kilmarnock victory. It was a bitter pill to swallow for Hearts as their play, especially in the first half, deserved better.

But Hearts displayed the mark of champions by refusing to buckle under the pressure, safe in the knowledge that the destiny of the League Championship lay in their own hands. As it transpired, Kilmarnock suffered an unexpected defeat by relegation-haunted Dunfermline at East End Park, which left Hearts requiring only one point from the final two games to clinch the title. The penultimate game was against St Mirren at Love Street on 16 April, the scene of the 1957/58 League Championship triumph. Would Hearts be able to repeat the feat? The fans were in no doubt about that and so were the players. Hearts knew that it would be just as difficult as it had been two years earlier but they were determined to wrap up the League title in Paisley. At times it hadn't been an easy season, with some ups and downs along the way, but this very experienced and battle-hardened team were not going to undo all that hard work now.

St Mirren: Walker, Wilson, Campbell, Doonan, Tierney, Thomson, Rodger, Bryceland, Baker, Gemmell, Miller.
Hearts: Marshall, Kirk, Thomson, Cumming, Milne, Higgins, Smith, Young, Bauld, McFadzean, Crawford.
Referee: Mr D. Massie, Dundee.

Three minutes after Willie Bauld had kicked off for a confident-looking Hearts, they looked a less cheerful side as Gordon Marshall picked the ball out of the net. With a perfectly placed header Tommy Bryceland had put the Saints ahead. But 3 minutes after that bombshell Hearts were back on level terms when Jim McFadzean scored. The goal settled the Tynecastle men, who began to play quality football, with Alex Young the architect of the attacking plans. St Mirren decided not to stand by idly and admire the Maroons' play and regained the lead through Tommy Gemmell. The goal set Love Street aflame as Hearts pulled out the last tricks in their repertoire in a bid to equalise, with Saints putting in a vast amount of effort for more goals. Fifteen minutes from the interval Ian Crawford equalised at the third attempt as the first two shots were blocked. Just on half time, St Mirren's Jim Rodger was sent off after a deliberate kick on George Thomson. Referee Massie had no hesitation in dismissing the 'saint' turned 'sinner'. Rodger ran off to a mixture of cheers and boos as the referee's whistle brought the first 45 minutes to a close. This game was not for the faint-hearted, with excitement and controversy in abundance. Down to ten men, St Mirren were expected to play defensively but the opposite happened. Led by Gerry Baker, brother of Hibs' Joe, they took the game to Hearts. It was no surprise when Baker, who was by now giving Jimmy Milne a torrid time, put them ahead with a superb goal. At great speed he had bobbed and weaved his way past the Hearts defenders before thundering a shot past Gordon Marshall. But the large Hearts travelling support roared their team on and the Hearts players responded by giving every ounce of energy they could find as they fought for every ball. It was at times frantic and then, after a quite incredible scramble in the goalmouth, Alex Young equalised. St Mirren protested the legitimacy of the goal but it stood. Then, astonishingly, Tommy Gemmell gave the 'Buddies' the lead once more when he scored with a penalty. Now the minutes were speeding away as Hearts applied tremendous pressure to salvage a point, a point that would give them the Championship. With seconds to go, Jim McFadzean struck the bar. Then Hearts claimed for a penalty when Gordon Smith was bundled in the box. The excitement was unbearable. Then the last chance. A Gordon Smith corner, a neat return by Ian Crawford to Willie Bauld, who turned and hit a thumping shot into the net with the last kick of the contest. Suddenly Bauld was being pummelled by the Hearts players as once more the King of Tynecastle turned up trumps again for his beloved club. The fans were on the field celebrating wildly as Mr Massie brought the game to an end, a game which will forever remain in the folklore of Heart of Midlothian. These were Tommy Walker's dignified words after the game:

We are proud to be Champions again and we are conscious of the new responsibility which has descended on us. We had a simple plan which had nothing to do with field tactics. It was simply that we would take each single game by itself and concentrate on it. We tried not to think of the future. We counted no points until they were won.

SEASON 1960/61

Given the previous season's success, the Hearts support looked forward to their side continuing where they had left off, but this was a season best forgotten as Hearts failed to come anywhere near the form of 1959/60. The team were very inconsistent to say the least, leading to Tommy Walker making changes to the line-up on a week-to-week basis in an attempt to find the right formation. Their form was alarming at times and morale seemed low. This wasn't helped by the unexpected transfer of Alex Young and George Thomson to Everton in late November 1960. Hearts completed the season empty-handed, finishing eighth in the League.

THE LEAGUE CUP

Hearts began with a visit from St Mirren and despite their territorial advantage, throughout the game Hearts had only a George Thomson penalty to show for their efforts. Near the end of a disappointing game the 'Buddies' equalised through Gerry Baker. A mid-week trip to Shawfield resulted in a 2-0 defeat as Clyde scored twice in the second half. There were grumblings by some of the fans with regards to a lacklustre performance by the Hearts forwards. That all changed on the Saturday, when Hearts defeated Motherwell 3-2 at Fir Park in another 'classic' between these great footballing sides. Hearts were two goals down after only 18 minutes but stormed back in the second half to level the scores. John Cumming scored the winner with a spectacular thirty-yard strike. The smiles were back on the faces of the maroon faithful, but not for long as they saw their team suffer a 3-1 defeat at Paisley the following week. However, following 6-2 and 2-1 wins over Clyde and Motherwell at Tynecastle, Hearts finished the section not only level on points with the 'Bully Wee' but also with an identical goal average. A play-off took place at Celtic Park on Monday 12 September. A combination of poor finishing by the Hearts forwards and resolute defending by Clyde resulted in a 2-1 defeat.

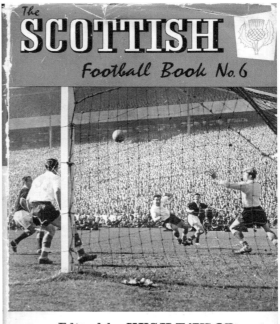

This page: *The Scottish Football Book 1960/61.*

Programme for the League Cup tie against St Mirren, 13 August 1960.

Programme for the League Cup tie against Motherwell, 3 September 1960.

Above left: Programme for the European Cup game against Benfica.

Above right: No match programme was issued for the return leg in Portugal but the game was highlighted in the club's magazine, which was issued weekly.

THE EUROPEAN CUP

Hearts' second venture into the European Cup ended just as quickly as the first did in 1958/59. They were beaten home and away, 2-1 and 3-0, by the Portuguese champions, Benfica. But there was no disgrace in these defeats as Benfica were a top-quality side packed with very skilful players. As it happened, Benfica went on to win the trophy after defeating Barcelona in the final.

THE LEAGUE CHAMPIONSHIP

Newly promoted St Johnstone were the visitors to Tynecastle on Wednesday 24 August when Hearts began their defence of the League Championship. Hearts gained a satisfactory 3-1 win, with goals from Ian Crawford, Gordon Smith and Jimmy Murray, Norrie Innes scoring for the Perth side. They followed this up with an emphatic 4-1 victory over Hibernian at Easter Road on 10 September. But after that their form dipped dramatically and it was not until 26 November that Hearts recorded another victory in the League, when Raith Rovers went down 1-0 at Tynecastle. Not only had their League form suffered but attendances at home had began to fall. A few days prior to the Raith Rovers fixture, the support were dealt a massive blow when the club announced that Alex Young and George Thomson were going to Merseyside to join Everton in a record deal thought to be in the region of £60,000. The fans were incensed as they watched their Championship side being dismantled bit by bit. It had been bad enough for them when Dave Mackay had gone to Spurs, but in the eyes of the support this transfer was unforgivable and they made their feelings known in the game against Raith Rovers. The team's form continued to be erratic going into the turn of the year.

The New Year didn't begin well, with a 2-1 defeat at Tynecastle by 'first footers' Hibernian at Tynecastle on 2 January. This was followed by another 2-1 reversal at East End Park as Dunfermline, under Jock Stein, began to make their mark on Scottish football. Only one League win was recorded in January, a 3-1 victory over Airdrie at Tynecastle.

Dalymount Park, Dublin, 7 May 1961 and Alex Young, now with Everton, scores the first of his two goals against the Republic of Ireland in a World Cup qualifying game. Charlie Hurley, ROI, and Ralph Brand are also in the photograph.

Alex scores the second goal in the 3-0 win. Ralph Brand, number 10, scored Scotland's third goal.

Alex Young was capped six times while playing for Hearts and is pictured here with John Cumming and Denis Law, being introduced to the Lord Provost of Glasgow. This was Alex's Scotland debut in a home international against England at Hampden on 9 April 1960. If there is such a thing as the 'perfect footballer', Alex Young would fill that role. His graceful style was a joy to behold and the Hearts support loved him with a passion. A tremendous goalscorer with either foot and excellent in the air, Alex menaced defences up and down the country as he glided past opposing defenders with consummate ease. He scored in a 2-1 win over Partick Thistle in his competitive debut on 27 August 1955, having joined Hearts from Newtongrange Star the previous year. By the time he left to join Everton in November 1960 Alex had won every major honour with Hearts. On Merseyside he was soon a fans' favourite.

Alex Young pictured at Hampden against Queens Park in a League game on 8 March 1955.

Programme for the visit of Hibernian, 2 January 1961. Crawford scored in the 2-1 defeat.

Above left: Programme for Hearts *v.* St Mirren Scottish Cup game.

Above right: Jimmy Murray in training with Andy Bowman. Despite making his League debut in April 1952, it took Jimmy a long time to establish himself as a first-team player. This was due to the fine form of the 'Terrible Trio' and Jimmy's appearances were mostly confined to the reserve side. In season 1956/57 he began to appear more regularly for the first team and became part of manager Walker's plans. In the following season, his form was outstanding as Hearts powered their way to the Championship. Murray's performances did not go unnoticed by the SFA selectors and he was chosen to travel to Sweden as part of Scotland's World Cup squad for the final stages of the competition. Jimmy netted Scotland's equalising goal in the 1-1 draw with Yugoslavia and has the distinction of scoring his country's first ever goal in the final stages of the World Cup. Murray's form for Hearts in the next two seasons never dipped as the team continued to dominate. Season 1960/61 was a transitional one for Hearts and Jimmy couldn't sustain his high standard. Consequently he was given a free transfer in May 1961 but Jimmy Murray will never be forgotten for the contribution he gave to Heart of Midlothian during his Tynecastle days.

THE SCOTTISH CUP

Tarff Rovers were the visitors to Tynecastle for the first round of Scottish Cup. Hearts showed no mercy as they stormed into the next round with a 9-0 victory. The only consolation for Tarff was the share of the 'gate' from an attendance of just over 13,000. The second round saw Hearts drawn away from home to face Kilmarnock at Rugby Park. Kilmarnock, who were formidable opponents, were chasing Rangers for the League Championship at that time but goals from Hamilton and Blackwood saw Hearts progress into the next stage of the competition with a hard-fought 2-1 victory. The next round was a tricky one as well – a visit to Maryhill on 25 February. Only three weeks earlier, Partick had inflicted Hearts with their biggest defeat of the season, a 4-1 drubbing in a League match at Firhill. Jimmy Murray gave his side a safe passage to the quarter-final stages with two first-half goals. Alex Wright replied for the 'Jags' near the end. Hearts were rewarded with a home tie against St Mirren and an excellent attendance of 34,325 turned up at Tynecastle for the encounter on 11 March. However, poor finishing and inspired goalkeeping by former Hearts favourite Jimmy Brown saw the 'Gorgie' men exit the competition by way of a Don Kerrigan first-half goal.

Because of some very poor performances, Hearts were now in free-fall and were being pulled into the relegation zone. But they stuck together and were undefeated in the remaining six games, enabling them to finish in eighth place, with thirty-four points from thirty-four games. The end of the season saw a few 'weel kent' faces depart Tynecastle. Jimmy Murray, Jimmy Milne, Wilson Brown and Gordon Smith were the most prominent players to leave as the team which had carried all before them in previous years began to break up. The end of a season is always tinged with a certain sadness when players leave clubs for a variety of reasons. This one was no exception as some of Tynecastle's favourite sons moved on, but they left thousands of fans with memories. Memories of halcyon days, with some superb team performances and individual displays during their stay in Gorgie.

SEASON 1961/62

New players in the shape of Willie Polland and Willie Wallace joined up at Tynecastle as Tommy Walker strived to get his side back to winning ways. Hearts had experimented with a 4-2-4 formation the previous season and now favoured this style of play. It wasn't popular with the fans but Walker viewed it as the way ahead. They reached the final of the League Cup but were beaten by Rangers after a replay. Their League form was very much up and down, finishing in sixth place, and this was reflected in attendances at Tynecastle in the latter part of the season as the fans stayed away in great numbers. Hearts took part in the Inter-Cities Fairs Cup but exited at the hands of Inter Milan in the second round, while their Scottish Cup hopes were brought to an end by Celtic in the third round of the competition, but in highly controversial circumstances.

THE LEAGUE CUP

The League Cup draw put Hearts into the same section as Raith Rovers, Kilmarnock and St Mirren. Full points were registered in the opening two games, with victories over Raith Rovers and Kilmarnock. The fans were less than impressed, however, when the following two games resulted in defeats at Love Street and Starks Park. To qualify for the final stages required full points from the remaining two games at home to Kilmarnock and St Mirren. The players responded admirably with 2-0 and 3-1 wins to stake their place in the quarter-finals. They defeated Hamilton Academical home and away 2-0 and 2-1 and were drawn against Stirling Albion in the semi-final, the venue being Easter Road. Stirling Albion had inflicted a 3-1 defeat on Hearts a few days earlier in a League game at Annfield but Tommy Walker made only one change for the semi-final, replacing Bobby Blackwood with Willie Bauld. Stirling took the lead just before half-time and with twenty minutes to go looked to be heading for the final as Hearts failed time after time to breech their rearguard. Then enter Willie Bauld. So often the saviour of Hearts, Willie did it again with a headed equaliser in the 71st minute. The game moved to extra time and the noise which greeted Willie Wallace's winner in the 104th minute could probably have been heard in Gorgie, such was the relief of the support. The other finalists were Rangers, who had only scraped through themselves in extra time in their semi-final against St Johnstone at Celtic Park.

In August 1961 Andy Bowman was freed to join Newport County. Andy joined Hearts from Chelsea in July 1955, making his competitive debut against Partick Thistle the following month in a League Cup game. Andy was a tireless worker in the midfield and didn't take 'many prisoners' with his style of play. He played a major part in the title wins of 1957/58 and 1959/60 and his efforts were appreciated by his team mates and fans alike.

Gordon Marshall collects the ball despite the attentions of Ralph Brand in the first match at Hampden.

Gordon Marshall joined Hearts in July 1956 from Balgreen Rovers and was then farmed out to Dalkeith Thistle for a short spell. Gordon made his competitive debut in November 1956 against Kilmarnock in a League match and very quickly made the goalkeeping position his own. Standing at over six feet in height, he was a commanding figure in goal and was excellent at dealing with cross balls. Gordon was a very confident goalkeeper and was the model of consistency during his Tynecastle career. He left Hearts in 1963 and joined Newcastle United. After five years on Tyneside he was transferred to Nottingham Forest before returning to Edinburgh in 1969, to Hibernian. Jock Stein then brought Gordon to Celtic in 1971. He had a short spell at Aberdeen before arriving at Arbroath. After a glittering career Gordon Marshall retired from the game in 1978.

THE LEAGUE CUP FINAL 1961/62

The League Cup final took place on 28 October at Hampden Park before almost 90,000 spectators. Going into the game, Hearts' form had been inconsistent. By contrast, the Ibrox men remained undefeated in the League and League Cup and were clear favourites to retain the trophy, having beaten Kilmarnock in the previous season's final.

Hearts: Marshall, Kirk, Holt, Cumming, Polland, Higgins, Ferguson, Elliot, Wallace, Gordon, Hamilton.
Rangers: Ritchie, Shearer, Caldow, Davis, Paterson, Baxter, Scott, McMillan, Millar, Brand, Wilson.
Referee: R. H. Davidson.

To describe this contest as tame would be an understatement; non-event would be a more appropriate description. The game was a huge disappointment as neither side played to their capabilities and there was little or no entertainment for the vast crowd. Hearts played their much criticised 4-2-4 formation, a system based on defence, and Rangers quite simply didn't have the key to unlock it. Rangers took the lead in 15 minutes with a goal that was bizarre to say the least. Millar of Rangers tried a shot at goal from all of thirty yards which Cumming and Polland for some reason didn't intercept, allowing the ball to pass them. It wasn't a particularly strong shot but Gordon Marshall was completely caught off-guard and the ball went into the net at his left-hand post. The game just sort of meandered along after that, with very few chances being created by either side, especially Hearts, who seemed content to play defensively. With 12 minutes remaining, the huge crowd were woken from their slumber when Hearts were awarded a penalty. Johnny Hamilton crossed into the box and as Alan Gordon went for the ball, referee Bobby Davidson adjudged that Rangers defender Harold Davis had pushed Gordon in the back. Davis looked suitably surprised and immediately the referee was confronted by less than happy Rangers defenders, none more than their goalie Billy Ritchie, who made as if to throw the ball at Davidson such was his anger. Fortunately for Ritchie, the proposed threat wasn't carried out in full. Davidson refused to change his decision and the calmest person on the field at that time, John Cumming, dispatched the ball into the net from the resultant penalty. The game at last came to life and went into extra time but despite chances for both teams it finished level. The following morning the Sunday newspapers had a field day as they lambasted both teams for their inept performance. The esteemed sports journalist Rex Kingsley's headline in the *Sunday Mail* was 'IF THIS IS 4-2-4 YOU CAN KEEP IT', in reference to Hearts' style of play.

THE LEAGUE CUP FINAL REPLAY

Because of both teams being involved in European games the replay was scheduled for Monday 4 December, but this was postponed because of a frozen Hampden pitch. The new date was fixed for a fortnight later.

Hearts: Cruickshank, Kirk, Holt, Cumming, Polland, Higgins, Ferguson, Davidson, Bauld, Blackwood, Hamilton.
Rangers: Ritchie, Shearer, Caldow, Davis, Baillie, Baxter, Scott, McMillan, Millar, Brand, Wilson.
Referee: R. H. Davidson.

A freezing fog, which had hung over Glasgow all day, threatened another postponement as kick-off time approached. As a result, the crowd of 47,552 was considerably lower than expected. Rangers began at a ferocious pace and playing with two men wide, Scott and Wilson, simply tore Hearts apart in the opening stages. The pressure paid off in 7 minutes when Millar headed them into the lead. But Hearts didn't fold and almost immediately they equalised through a quite brilliant Norrie Davidson header. Any hopes that Hearts nurtured of keeping the game tight

Jim Cruickshank.

Jim Baxter runs over to congratulate Ian McMillan after he had scored in the replay.

very quickly evaporated as Jim Baxter took over. Baxter simply ran the show with his skill and vision, and quite honestly few teams could have coped with his artistry that cold winter's evening. Further goals by Brand and McMillan in the 15th and 19th minutes put the game beyond Hearts. In the second half Rangers hit the woodwork on four occasions as the Tynecastle men tried to keep the score at a respectable level. To put the result into perspective, it should be understood that this was an excellent Rangers side at that period in history. Orchestrated by Jim Baxter, they were once again dominating Scottish football as the balance of power moved once again from east to west. The one crumb of comfort for the Hearts fans as they departed Hampden that foggy night had been the performance of Jim Cruickshank in goal. Jim had replaced the injured Gordon Marshall for the replay and this had been his only outing for the first team that season. But he had played like a veteran in the game, especially in the second half, when time after time he brought off saves which were sometimes breathtaking. Cruickshank continued to be Marshall's understudy before making the goalkeeping position his own in 1963. 'Cruikie', as he was known to the Hearts support, became a cult figure down Tynecastle way because of his bravery and unstinting efforts to give his all for the team. His association with Hearts ended on a sour note when the club refused to recognise his seventeen years' service with a testimonial game and he left in 1977. Jim had a short spell at Dumbarton before retiring from the game the following year.

In a sparsely populated San Siro stadium, Willie Wallace challenges the Inter keeper.

INTER-CITIES FAIRS CUP

Hearts travelled to Belgium to play Union Gilliose in the first round of the competition and recorded a fine 3-1 victory with a Bobby Blackwood goal and a double from Norrie Davidson. Willie Wallace and Robin Stenhouse completed the task at Tynecastle the following week. Inter Milan came to Edinburgh on 6 November for the next round and simply 'parked the bus' at Tynecastle. The Italians allowed Hearts to have a lot of the ball and were content to defend while trying to catch them on the break. They did just that with twelve minutes to the break when a slip by Polland allowed Humberto to take advantage and score. In the second half Hearts had no answer to Inter's hugely talented players, who flew home to Milan with a one-goal advantage. A fortnight later in the San Siro Stadium former Aston Villa player Gerry Hitchins scored twice as Hearts went down 4-0 to a side who were a class apart.

THE LEAGUE CHAMPIONSHIP

Hearts blew hot and cold during the League season. Some very good performances were followed by ones which at times were mediocre. Again Tommy Walker chopped

Willie Bauld made his competitive debut on 9 October 1948 in a League Cup game against East Fife, scoring a hat-trick in a 6-1 win. Before the season's end he found the net another twenty-one times, including two more hat-tricks. The game against the Fifers was the first time that Alfie Conn, Willie and Jimmy Wardhaugh had begun a competitive game together and 'The Terrible Trio' was born. Little did the Hearts support imagine the joy all three would bring to the stands and terraces during their time together as they netted around 950 first team goals between them and struck fear into opposing teams the length and breadth of the country.

Willie's career as a centre-forward started off in his school days. When he came of age to enter the school team, everyone had a position, except Willie. The centre-forward position was vacant and that was how he came to play as a 'centre' – more by luck than good judgement. From school football he graduated to Boys Brigade football when he was 15 years old and it was there that Musselburgh Union first showed an interest. But their interest soon waned, their departing words being, 'He's nae guid.' Jimmy Train of Edinburgh Waverley must have spotted something in the young Bauld for very soon he had him in Waverley's line-up. His first game for them was against none other than Musselburgh Union. Very quickly Musselburgh saw the error of their ways and they signed Bauld, who turned out for them over the next six months.

All this time Sunderland's representative, Walter Scott, had been following Bauld's progress and the English side signed him as a provisional player. From Union he moved to Musselburgh Athletic and before long Sunderland sent a letter stating that Willie was their registered player. But by now Willie wasn't keen on going to England and it was only testing work by some officials that saw his registration cancelled. Hearts offered him terms, after ground work by scout Tam Fraser, and Willie put pen to paper with Club Secretary Jimmy Kean and Mrs Kean witnessing his signature. He was farmed out to Newtowngrange Star for six months before ligament trouble side-lined him. Hearts then arranged for him to play with Edinburgh City, who played in what was known then as Scottish 'C' Division, and his time at the Pilton ground helped to knock some of the rough edges off his game. Willie carried a powerful shot but it was his heading ability which made him stand out from the rest, whether it was knocking balls into the path of Conn or Wardhaugh or bulleting headers into the net. Surprisingly, Bauld was only capped on three occasions for his country.

During his playing career Willie suffered many injuries which eventually took their toll and at the end of the 1961/62 season he retired from football. His last ever League goal for Hearts came in a 2-1 victory over Third Lanark on 7 February 1962 at Tynecastle. The Edinburgh Evening News then ran a competition titled the 'Willie Bauld Tribute' with a prize of £5 going to the person who penned the best letter in respect of the Tynecastle legend. The response was immense. The batches of letters received from followers of Rangers, Celtic and Hibs as well as Hearts fans testified to Willie's popularity.

Willie Bauld died on 11 March 1977, aged only 49. On the day of his funeral many lined Gorgie Road to pay their last respects to 'The King'. They stood together in silence, each with their own memories of Willie, as the cortege slowly passed his beloved Tynecastle Park on its way to Warriston Crematorium.

and changed his team to no avail, with attendances falling as the fans became even more disgruntled. The two victories over arch rivals Hibs in the League, 4-2 at Tynecastle in September and 4-1 at Easter Road in January, helped to dispel the gloom a bit. The League began with a 2-2 draw with St Mirren, but maximum points were dropped in away games against Dunfermline, Dundee and Stirling Albion. Some of these points were philanthropically presented to say the least, and by the end of October Hearts sat mid-table, with nine points from eight games.

By the end of January Hearts were more or less out of the race for the League title, having taken only twenty-one points from twenty-eight games. Dundee, who had already completed the 'double' over Hearts, had emerged as the form team and deservedly led the League table. Under manager Bob Shankly they had put together some very impressive displays, including a 5-1 defeat of Rangers at Ibrox earlier in the season with Alan Gilzean scoring four of the goals. In turn, Hearts had only the Scottish Cup to look forward to.

THE SCOTTISH CUP

After receiving a bye in the first round of the cup, Hearts made the short journey to the border town of Innerleithen to play Vale of Leithen. The Tynecastle men eased themselves safely into the next round with a 5-0 win. The third round saw them drawn against Celtic at Tynecastle. On Saturday 17 February a crowd of 35,045, Hearts' biggest attendance of the season, were inside Tynecastle to see what can be best described as a good old-fashioned cup-tie played out in front of them. John Divers put Celtic ahead after just 12 minutes but a Bobby Blackwood goal in the 21st minute cancelled it out. In the second half Hearts were well on top and it was no surprise when Johnny Hamilton put them ahead with 19 minutes of the game remaining. A few minutes later Steve Chalmers levelled the game for Celtic and shortly after that another goal by Divers put them ahead. Hearts refused to lie down and Danny Paton made it 3-3 with 8 minutes to the final whistle. But more drama was to follow when referee Bobby Davidson awarded Celtic a controversial penalty kick with 4 minutes to go. Gordon Marshall saved Pat Crerand's penalty to a tremendous roar from the Hearts support. Joy quickly turned to anger when Davidson, for reasons best known to himself, ordered that the penalty be retaken. Crerand made no mistake this time and Hearts exited the tournament.

The defeat by Celtic in the Scottish Cup took its toll on the team and in the remaining ten League fixtures they recorded only two wins, one of them being the last game of the season, at Tannadice, when they defeated Dundee United 1-0 courtesy of a Jim Rodger goal. This victory enabled them to finish in sixth place with thirty-eight points, a massive sixteen points behind the League Champions, Dundee. The end of that season saw Willie Bauld depart Tynecastle to retire from the game, bringing the end to an illustrious career.

SEASON 1962/63

The League Cup was won for the fourth time and overall the side had a more settled look and a greater balance throughout. Willie Hamilton arrived from Middlesborough but unfortunately missed five of the sectional League Cup games because of injury; however, very soon he made his presence felt. League performances were a massive improvement on the previous season and consequently attendances began to rise, with Hearts well placed in the League table. But then fate stepped in; Scotland became gripped in the worst winter the country had endured since 1947. From the beginning of November snow had been falling and by early January blizzards were sweeping the country. It became known as the 'big freeze' as Scotland shivered and the weather took its toll. The football calendar was completely wiped out from the middle of January till early March. The enforced close-down had an adverse effect on the side and when the League got underway again the team seemed a bit lethargic. The cutting edge had gone from the play and, more worrying, Willie Hamilton, who had been a revelation earlier in the season, appeared to have lost his appetite for the game. In the Scottish Cup, Hearts defeated Forfar in the first round only to go out to Celtic 3-1 at Celtic Park on 6 March. This was Hearts' first game since 15 December.

THE LEAGUE CUP

Celtic, Dundee United and League Champions Dundee were grouped with Hearts for the sectional ties. It was not the easiest of sections to be in and the opening game at Celtic Park proved that when Hearts went down 3-1. Bobby Murdoch gave Celtic a 7th-minute lead but Danny Paton equalised 15 minutes later. Two early second-half goals by Charlie Gallagher and John Hughes finished the contest. Hearts then registered two good wins over Dundee United at Tynecastle and Dundee at Dens Park. This brought them level with Celtic on four points at the halfway stage and the visit of Celtic to Tynecastle on 25 August became vital to both sides in terms of qualifying for the quarter-finals. In front of a crowd of 33,000 Danny Paton put Hearts ahead and by half-time Willie Wallace had doubled the lead. Five minutes into the second period, Hearts were awarded a penalty when Billy McNeill fouled Norrie Davidson in the box. Willie Wallace made no mistake from the spot. Bobby

Murdoch reduced the leeway in the 60th minute and a goal by John Hughes in the dying minutes of the game made the score a bit more respectable for the Glasgow side, but no one could deny that this was a richly deserved victory for Hearts. But then Hearts contrived to make it difficult for themselves in qualifying by going down 2-0 at Tannadice the following Wednesday. The same evening Celtic defeated Dundee 3-0. Hearts and Celtic were back on level points, with the 'Hoops' having the superior goal average. Hearts had to win their final game against Dundee and hope that Dundee United would take something from their game with Celtic. Hearts did their bit by beating Dundee 2-0 and then the final score came through from Tannadice: a 0-0 draw.

Hearts' quarter-final opponents were Morton, with the first leg being at Cappielow. Hearts won this one 3-0 and the next week completed the task with a 3-1 victory at home. St Johnstone were comprehensively defeated 4-0 at Easter Road in the semi-finals on 10 October to secure the Gorgie men's place in the final, where they would meet Kilmarnock, who had beaten Rangers 3-2 in the other semi-final.

THE LEAGUE CUP FINAL 1962/63

Going into the final on 27 October, Hearts were in fine form, being undefeated in the League. Kilmarnock's form had also been impressive, apart from a 1-0 reversal at Dens Park the week prior to the final. The teams had already drawn 2-2 in a League match at Rugby Park on 13 October, so the scene was set for what was hoped would be an entertaining game between two well-matched teams. It would be a game filled with excitement and controversy. Approaching the weekend of the final, the Cuban Missile Crisis was at its height. The world waited with bated breath as nuclear oblivion threatened Mother Earth's inhabitants as Russia and the USA squared up to each other. But the followers of Hearts and Kilmarnock weren't really concerned too much about trivialities such as nuclear fallouts and world disasters as they made their way to Hampden that wet and windy Saturday. No, they had a much more important contest on their minds – the League Cup final.

The team line-ups were:

Hearts: Marshall, Polland, Holt, Cumming, Barry, Higgins, Wallace, Paton, Davidson, W. Hamilton, J. Hamilton.
Kilmarnock: McLaughlan, Richmond, Watson, O'Connor, McGrory, Beattie, Brown, Black, Kerr, McInally, McIlroy.
Referee: Mr Tom Wharton.

The following is a report of the game taken from Hugh Taylor's *Scottish Football Book*:

Hearts won the toss and Kilmarnock wearing their impressive new modern strip of vertical blue-and-white stripes, had to face the breeze. From the kick-off however they opened with vigorous attacking play that chased any thoughts of a hoodoo and had Hearts' defence in trouble. Indeed, if it hadn't been for the greasy surface and slippery ball, the Ayrshire team might have been two goals up in the first three minutes.

From the kick off, wily centre forward Andy Kerr sent a fine through ball inside Roy Barry. Darting through was Bertie Black. He took the ball and with all Ayrshire roaring, he beat goal-keeper Marshall – then lost possession. Black fell. So did Marshall. The ball rolled loose. John Cumming, off balance, just managed to hook the ball to safety. But Kilmarnock were not happy at all and claimed that Black had been held by Marshall as he tried to rise.

But they wasted little time in protesting – and were soon back threatening the Hearts goal. Over came a cross from Kerr. Again Black had the ball. Again he slipped – and thankful Hearts scrambled the ball away once again.

Powerful Kilmarnock were roaring in for an early kill in this inspired start and in seven minutes the Edinburgh defence was in a tangle after Brian McIlroy had made a fine opening. Once again they got the break of the ball.

What an iron grip Kilmarnock had taken. McIlroy was bursting through on his own when he was stopped by a gallant last-ditch tackle by Higgins.

At last Hearts moved into the attacking picture and Norrie Davidson, that sharp-shooting, agile little centre forward from the north of Scotland, raised the first Edinburgh cheer. From twenty yards he hit a great shot and wee Sandy McLaughlan had to sail through the air like an acrobat to make a spectacular save.

Already it was proving a gruelling, exciting match, even though mistakes were frequent on the slippery surface. Although Hearts, prompted by the skilled passes of Willie Hamilton, had survived their shaky opening and were showing more inspired attacking moves, Kilmarnock still held the edge and Marshall had to move smartly out of his goal to stop Kerr.

And then, in the twenty-sixth minute, Hamilton showed just why he was the new pin-up boy of Tynecastle. Hearts were still under constant pressure. Right-winger Willie Wallace was back helping his defenders, back on their heels. To give his colleagues breathing space, Wallace slung a long ball from the heart of his defensive area. The ball landed at Hamilton's feet. Almost casually, the inside man took it under control. Off he meandered. Away on the left, he lured centre half Jackie McGrory, beat him, and cut back a glorious pass across goal. Norrie Davidson was storming in and he smartly whipped the ball into the back of the net from close range.

A moment of magic for the Maroons, brilliant opportunism indeed, a goal beautifully made by Hamilton. But what a sickener for Kilmarnock, who had been so much on top.

The shock was reflected in their play. Hearts' tails were up and they began at last to dictate play, with Willie Hamilton the cool maestro causing most of the worry in the Ayrshire defence. And Kilmarnock often didn't look happy as Hearts set up a slick Hampden glide towards McLaughlan's goal.

Still Kilmarnock were fighting magnificently and in one quick thrust McInally might have scored. But he held on too long and Barry stepped in to clear. And then we noticed that Kilmarnock's hoodoo had swooped again. McInally was limping badly. He had injured his foot.

Just as Hearts' outlook became brighter, however, the doughty men of Rugby Park made a valiant effort. Suddenly a Barry miskick had Hearts in trouble. McIlroy pounced on the ball and dashed in menacingly. Luckily, Holt crashed in to drag the ball from the winger's foot as he was about to tap the ball over the line.

The half finished with Marshall making a glorious save from a Beattie shot. Kilmarnock had been out of luck – but they could blame their forwards for failing to cash in on the chances made. Hearts with far less of the play, had seized their opportunity brilliantly. That was the main difference between the sides.

In the second half, Kilmarnock had to move the limping McInally to outside-right, with Hugh Brown at inside left. Big Mac was obviously crippled but what a trier he was. On one occasion he raced past surprised Hearts defenders and gave them a fright with a fine shot which Marshall did well to stop.

Soon after this McIlroy miskicked near goal and was also at fault when he failed to get the ball across to Kerr, in scoring position.

Despite these attempts, however, Hearts in the second half had more drive in attack and greater cohesion all round in this bruising, stamina-sapping final. They had at last taken command of the game and only desperate defence and heroics by Sandy McLaughlan prevented the Tynecastle team from adding to the score.

Then, as the rain pelted from the lowering skies and the Hampden lights were switched on twenty minutes from the end, Kilmarnock, seemingly down and out, well beaten, crippled, their goal-takers off form, suddenly mounted dramatic attacks – a series of sweeping, fierce, gallant fight-backs that will go down in soccer history.

But credit Hearts with pluck, with a well-drilled defence. Young Barry was outstanding. So was goalkeeper Marshall. And as the seconds ticked away Kilmarnock became more and more frustrated as wild attack after wild attack was easily repulsed.

Then came the dramatic end – and to this day Kilmarnock fans swear it was a goal that Frank Beattie scored. But the history book has a different story. And Hearts won the League Cup.

It is true they played the better football and nothing could dim the lustre of Willie Hamilton, the outstanding figure of a great match. His ball work was superb, his precise passes the mainspring of most of the Hearts attacks.

It was a sporting final, exciting all the time, and it proved that Hearts and Kilmarnock had moved into the forefront of Scottish soccer, strong, skilled teams able to match the best in Europe.

But what a pity Mr Wharton, a fine referee, was not allowed to give his opinion of what had happened at that disputed goal.

Surely the time has come for the removal of the gag on the referee – an outdated rule in these days when football is really show business, top entertainment, with the paying public entitled to know what is going on.

Bedlam ensues as the Kilmarnock players surround the referee following Frank Beattie's disallowed goal. Billy Higgins on the left appears to be applauding Mr Wharton for the decision.

Obviously the major talking point after the game was Frank Beattie's headed goal in the dying seconds being chalked off for an infringement. Press photos were inconclusive but Mr Wharton had spotted a hand being used and had blown for the foul before the ball had crossed the line. But try telling that to Kilmarnock fans. To this day there are still rumblings going on in deepest Ayrshire with regards to 'that goal'.

Nonetheless, Hearts had deservedly won the trophy for the fourth time in their history.

THE LEAGUE CHAMPIONSHIP

A hat-trick by Norrie Davidson in a 3-1 win over Dundee got Hearts off to the best possible start. It got better when another hat-trick, this time by Danny Paton, helped to sink Hibs at Easter Road 4-0. John Cumming was the other scorer. Further victories against Airdrie, Partick Thistle and Queen of the South were recorded before points were dropped in drawn games away from home against Dunfermline and Kilmarnock. But it was back to winning ways with a hard-earned 2-1 victory over Motherwell at Tynecastle on 20 October. In the week following the League Cup final Falkirk gave Hearts their first League defeat with a 2-0 win at Brockville. The side then went on a seven-game unbeaten run which put them into third place in the League, only three points behind the leaders Rangers, by mid-December; and then the snow arrived.